The Walcheren Expedition

The Walcheren Expedition

The Experiences of
a British Officer of the 81st Regt.
During the Campaign
in the Low Countries of 1809

Anonymous

The Walcheren Expedition
by Anonymous

First published under the title
Letters from Flushing

Leonaur is an imprint
of Oakpast Ltd

Copyright in this form © 2008 Oakpast Ltd

ISBN: 978-1-84677-636-6 (hardcover)
ISBN: 978-1-84677-635-9 (softcover)

http://www.leonaur.com

Publisher's Notes

In the interests of authenticity, the spellings, grammar and place names used have been retained from the original editions.

The opinions of the authors represent a view of events in which he was a participant related from his own perspective, as such the text is relevant as an historical document.

The views expressed in this book are not necessarily those of the publisher.

Contents

Advertisement 7

Letters &c. &c. 9

Advertisement

The public have been deeply and justly interested, in the progress and issue of that grand expedition to the Continent which was expected to operate as a diversion in favour of our allies, to vindicate the wrongs, and assert the glory of Great Britain.

The Author of the following letters wrote them at the periods at which they are severally dated, to gratify some dear and intimate friends in London; and, finding that they have afforded a flattering degree of satisfaction beyond the circle for which they were originally intended, he has submitted to the persuasions of his friends, and consented to give them to the public.

All the claim they possess to general notice arises from their fidelity, and that the events were, described at the moment they occurred. The reader may in consequence gratify his curiosity by the fireside in an equal degree with those who accompanied the expedition, without partaking of their privations, or sharing in those hazards and sickness which befell nearly the whole of the army.

Those who are anxious to solve the problem, whether Great Britain can maintain its conquest, and whether it is worth the expense of retention; will find in the work data on which to form accurate conclusions.

Bedford Square
October 1809

Letters &c. &c.

Letter 1

Ramsgate, July 27, 1809.

My Dear Sir,

I am still at Ramsgate, but expect every moment to be ordered on board. My companions in arms are almost all in their several berths, and my division is to be embarked either tomorrow or the following day. In the meantime, all the officers who yet remain on shore have enough to do in executing little friendly offices for their companions who have embarked. Every boat brings us some errand or other. Nothing can be more social, and indeed necessarily so, than a military life. All restraints and ceremonies which the laws of fashion require in social life, give way before our military necessities; and no one is so much a stranger in a regiment, but what he may take any liberty he pleases with the time and trouble of a brother officer. If you are unfortunate enough to have any selfish friend, send him into the army. A siege or an embarkation will soon teach him the policy as well as the duty of mutual sacrifices, and in exchange of services.

You will very readily imagine that this bustle of embarkation gives an unusual life to Ramsgate. To say the truth, Ramsgate no longer resembles the same place. It reminds me of a country lady in a London rout. Everything is bustle, agitation, running backwards and forwards. The place is full of the wives, friends, and daughter of the officers about to embark. We hourly meet many lovely faces either actually suffused in tears, or with evident marks that they have but just taken the last embrace of some beloved objects. How happy must, those be who are thus beloved by those angelic figures! This reflection suggests itself every moment. There is much of distress, however, in this spectacle; many of our bravest men seem to have left the better part of their hearts behind them. It was a saying of Sir John Moore, that a soldier had nothing to do with a wife, and he frequently expressed a wish that no married man would select his regiment. Sir John Moore, though as elegant a man as was in the army, had very little attachment for the ladies. He truly loved his profession, and placed all his pleasure in the good discipline of his men.

You ask me what is my opinion of our present; commander in chief. There is an old proverb, that "walls have ears," and perhaps there are some things which should not be committed to letters. An officer, moreover, has perhaps no right to speak with too much freedom of his commander: so much, however, I will say, that I could wish the Earl would be more active in putting his talents forth. He is certainly a man of abilities, he thinks solidly, and writes extremely well; but it is not very easy to arouse him into exertion; he is indolent beyond any man I have ever seen.

At the present moment he bustles about with some appearance of alacrity; but it is evidently only a fit and a start, and all of us begin to apprehend a relapse. If you pass his window in his hours of leisure, you will invariably see him yawning, or with a book, over which he is sleeping. To sum up all, however, and perhaps to compensate for all, he has the reputation of being as honest a man as Heaven ever formed; he is the perfect gentleman, moreover, in his manners and deportment, and, as I have said before, whatever he does, he does well. If his activity were but equal to his talents, he would be inferior to none of our most celebrated generals.

I must add one more circumstance, which is highly honourable to the memory of his deceased brother. As the brother of the immortal Pitt, his appointment has given universal satisfaction amongst all the officers; and I do really believe that, under this impelling principle, they would do more for him than for any general in the service. I can scarcely describe to you the enthusiasm with which the good people of Ramsgate flock around the brother of Pitt, and the son of Chatham. There is some reward even in this world for good deeds and a well-merited reputation. How different, however, is the testimony which is paid to the brother of Pitt, from that which is extended to the brother of ———. Whence is this difference? Alas! The answer is so easy— Earl Chatham has nothing about him which can counterweigh against the honour of his illustrious relative—he is worthy both of Pitt and Chatham.

The brother of ——— phoh! I'll say no more about him, except that it seems as if Heaven intended to teach us the vanity of all earthly honours, by shewing us how contemptible they may become when transmitted to those who are unworthy of them, from the crowded state of the town, nothing can be more unpleasant than our situation. Many of us are compelled to hunt for a night's lodging, by which I mean, that we have to walk for it into some of the neighbouring villages; and very lucky are we if half a score of us can obtain permission to occupy a single room amongst us. Where did you obtain your information that the people of those towns and villages make it a point of duty to consult our convenience and comfort, and are all ready with their best services to assist and accommodate us? No such things my friend! As far as our money goes, they will assist us on being well paid; but even in these points their extortion is horrible. But as to any gratuitous services, any kindnesses, we have not to thank them, for one exertion on our behalf.

As to the destination of our expedition, it is by this time, I believe, tolerably well known to both our friends and foes. This is one of our secret expeditions, the precise object of which is known to all the world. No one, however, can justly be blamed for this. If anything be impossible, it is for England to have a secret expedition, The nature of the preparations, the multitude of persons necessarily in the secret, very intelligibly point out the purpose of the armament; and accordingly a fleet is no sooner collected in any of our outports, than every inhabitant of the town will whisper to you its destination,

The objects of the present expedition, whatever they may be, are here universally stated to be comprehended in the line of the Scheldt. I need not inform you that Government have received frequent information of the defenceless state of the Dutch Netherlands, as well as the progressive creation of a naval force behind the shelter of the Islands of Zealand. With respect to the state of the country, it has been repeatedly intimated to the Ministry that the Netherlands were so utterly destitute of all soldiers, that a force landed on the banks of the Scheldt, might penetrate to Antwerp, and thence to Ghent, without any serious resistance.

Our Government, desirous of ascertaining the truth of this information, have repeatedly instructed our cruisers to land small detachments; and the issue has invariably been such as confirmed the previous reports. In one single instance Lord W. Stuart penetrated nearly fifty miles inwards, and returned, merely with his boat's crew. With respect to the force actually in the Scheldt, the enquiries of Government had the same result. The vicinity of the forests, and the perfect and uninterrupted tranquillity of the workmen, had enabled the French to effect much; and if the same causes were allowed to continue, more was still to be dreaded. Under these circumstances, as I understand, the expedition is going to make an attack on the islands at the mouth of the Scheldt; and if we should succeed, we are to pass down the river, and destroy the French ships and flotilla at Sanvliet and Antwerp. You now know as much of the expedition as is known here. The military are very cautious what they say upon this delicate point; but the townspeople have no hesitation in publicly expressing what they know and think.

Ramsgate is so much changed within these four last years, that in your next visit to it, you will scarcely recognise it as the same. These bathing towns remind one very strongly of upstarts.

They grow saucier as they grow richer; and every day is distinguished by some pew caprice, and some new extravagance. This is the case with Ramsgate. Twenty years since it was a humble, modest, unaffected country hamlet, and received its annual visitants with respect for their superior rank, and with gratitude for the solid benefits which they derived from them. Everything is now sadly changed. Everything is double the price that it bears in London; extortion is practised in every shape, and the townspeople seem to have no thought but how to fleece the visitors. You would really be astonished at the enormous price which it demanded for the vilest lodging.

If a fowl is brought to market, it is kept till the latest possible hour, in order, by competition of buyers, to extort the utmost possible price. This spirit of squeezing is carried so far, that if you meet a cowboy in the fields, and ask him how many cows he attends, he will expect a shilling for his answer, and look savagely if you put nothing, in his extended hat. A fellow, shewed me the road to St. Peter's, about two miles from hence, and seemed disappointed when I gave him only a shilling though he did not walk a hundred yards. I do really believe that the people of Ramsgate would sell salt-water if there were any customers for it

Ramsgate is certainly much improved within the last three years in its buildings and its accommodations; in every other respect it has been retrograde. It is no longer a place of recess or retreat. It has lost its honesty with its simplicity. It has become a fashionable place, and adopted everything which fashion brings in its train. The lower orders of people are alternately servile and insolent, and the tradesmen have no rule but to get as much as they can.

As to the country round. Ramsgate, nothing can be more delightful. The Isle of Thanet is perfectly unenclosed; but at every mile, or half mile, is a grove or knoll of trees, from the midst of which appears a village church; the houses; moreover, are intermixed in the trees, so as to constitute the most picturesque scenery in the world. The morning walks of the visitors are usually directed towards some of these villages; and the humble peasantry, and lower class of farmers, frequently experience the liberality of their opulent visitors. In most of these houses milk, strawberries, and raspberries are to be procured at the proper season; but I am sorry to have to add, that the extortion of the town has spread into the neighbourhood, and that even a passing refreshment at a village house must be dearly paid for.

From the first appearance of the Isle of Thanet, any one would conclude that it was not very healthy; and, from the result of my enquiries on the spot, I conceive myself enabled to say, that in winter it is not so, and that the Kentish fever extends to this Isle. The Isle of Thanet is what the sailors call elevated table-ground amidst surrounding marshes. It is bounded on every sides by low grounds, the exhalations of which must necessarily be very unhealthy. The practical inference I would deduce from this circumstance is, that the visitor of Ramsgate should not protract his stay beyond the last week in October. When the November mists and rains come on, Ramsgate is equally disagreeable and unwholesome. The townspeople are aware of this; and accordingly after October, every necessary of life becomes as cheap as in the northern parts of Wales. You would no longer think yourself in the same country.

Turkeys, which have been hitherto sold for a guinea, are then five, six, or seven shillings; ducks a shilling each, and fowls equally reasonable, The flag of distress, as it is termed, appears on every window; and in the hopes of alluring some Cockney, "Lodgings on the lowest Terms," is displayed at every house.

I have just learned an important particular with respect to this expedition. You may remember that some years since General Dumourier was in high favour with the British Government, and. more particularly with Mr. Pitt, whose main foible it was to listen too confidently to foreigners and emigrants. General Dumourier was almost daily with Mr. Pitt, and was admitted by him to the most implicit confidence, The Court of Vienna were daily importuning Sir Author Paget to induce the English Ministry to make a diversion, and proposed the coast of Holland. A Council was at length held on the subject, and a memoir of General Dumourier's submitted to it. On the contents of this memoir our present expedition is founded. It is necessary, however, to add, that the general gave it as his decided opinion, that no such expedition could succeed; that Holland was infinitely too strong for any probable chance to such an effort, and that the Dutch had been so weaned by changes, and had already suffered so much, that it was idle to expect their co-operation; that the original success of the French was to be imputed to the strong party which their principles and professions had made, and more particularly to the universal hostility which had been provoked against the family of the *Stadtholder*.

You will be surprised that our expedition has been undertaken in the teeth and front of this opinion. General Dumourier was undoubtedly one of the most able of the French generals; he had travelled much, and had meditated on what he had seen. I know not, indeed, whence it has happened that so strange an error has prevailed with respect to this extraordinary, man. He has been vilified as a traitor to his country. General Dumourier merely consulted his self-defence in his escape from the French commissioners. I do not believe that he ever indulged a thought of restoring monarchy to France.

The author of this expedition is Lord Castlereagh; his reputation is particularly pledged upon its success. According to very probable report, it is not in much favour with the other division of the Cabinet. Neither you nor I meddle much in politics; but you may perhaps deem what I am about to inform you of, as not an unimportant point of intelligence. It is confidently reported, that the Cabinet is divided between Mr. Canning, and the Duke of Portland on one side, and Lord Liverpool and Lord Castlereagh on the other. Lord Castlereagh is protected by Lord Liverpool, and Mr. Perceval sides with them.

This is the political gossip of the day. How far it may be true or false, events will shew. The Cabinet, in the meantime, is believed to be equally divided and the event perhaps waits the success of the expedition. If Lord Castlereagh succeeds in Holland, he succeeds in England; if defeated in Holland, you will have him put out of the Cabinet, and Canning will become paramount. It is certainly not right, or at least such is my opinion, that those should have such a share in the acts of the Cabinet, who have no personal presence or responsibility there. You will understand to what I allude hereafter.

Before I conclude this letter, I must mention one additional point with respect to Ramsgate, which will excite some surprise in you. It is a circumstance very honourable to the manners of the fashionable world; and that is, that the visitors of Ramsgate are infinitely more attentive to their religious duties than whilst in town. The churches are crowded on a Sunday, and the deportment of the assembly is such as becomes them when in the presence of their Maker. This, at least, is one good of their retreat into the country, that they find leisure for the discharge of duties which they forget amidst the levities of the town. I am so pleased with this trait, that, in consideration of it, I will excuse them many follies. I shall never despair of their morals or of their hearts, in whom this religious principle is not extinct.

Confess that I have written you a long letter. Tomorrow we embark. The orders have been this moment given. We are all in high spirits; and, to do justice to the people of Ramsgate, whom I have been all along abusing, they do not seem wanting in patriotism. Everyone anticipates the full success of our expedition; everyone predicts it; and when our force is considered, their predictions may not seem to require much sagacity. The wind is varying; but, according to the sailors, will before tomorrow fix in the point which we want. *Adieu!* With compliments to all, and respectful remembrance to your mother.

Yours &c.

Letter 2

East Capelle, July 30, 1809.
My Dear Sir,
When I last wrote to you, I informed you that peremptory orders were given that every officer should immediately go on

board his respective ship. If you have ever been in a port when this order has been given, you may recall to your mind the infinite bustle which it creates. Military men are not the most thoughtful in the world; and it very seldom happens but that on these occasions they are taken by surprise. Though every one of us had expected this order momentarily, we were not on that account the more prepared for it. One man had his trunk to cord; another had to procure money for his bills.

Now I have mentioned this last circumstance, I most not omit to add, that this want of cash was the most horrible inconvenience incident upon our haste. You would scarcely credit me, were I to relate half the extortion on one side, and the sacrifice on the other, which has been made and sustained, in this exchange of our Bank of England notes for gold and silver. Fifteen shillings for a pound note is considered as a moderate price; and some of, my friends have sold theirs for ten. Surely in any future Expedition something will be contrived to prevent this extortion. Cash, at any rate, must be had, as we cannot expect that our notes will pass current in Zealand, Will this inconvenience be permanent?

The pier, the hills, and the sands presented a very interesting spectacle, "Surely England," said a foreigner, upon his first arrival among us, "is the land of angels!" You would have acknowledged the justice of this exclamation, if you had seen the number of lovely women who were assembled to witness our departure. Every face had the traits of a deep concern in our welfare. All reserve was banished in the feelings of the moment. The most lovely girls waved their hands and handkerchiefs to all who passed them, whether strangers or acquaintance. Most of these women were in tears. May their husbands, fathers, and lovers return to them, to reap in their affection the reward of their bravery! The more I see of this interesting spectacle, the more do I become a convert to Sir John Moore's maxim—that a soldier should have nothing to do with a wife. And yet I think that some of these wives are too precious luxuries for us contentedly to give the monopoly of them to you non-military gentlemen.

About four in the afternoon of the 28th, we were all, in our boats, and, waving our hats in the air, in return to the salutations of our countrymen, sought our respective ships. It was not without some difficulty that we made them, the crowd and bustle being extreme. Innumerable boats still plied us, in order to sell some of their commodities; and so thoughtless were we, that, although cash was so scarce, and our voyage could not possibly be longer than the night, we bought of everyone.

Upon reaching our vessels, there was still a greater bustle than in making our way to them. The men, having been some days on board, had already enough of the sea, and were seemingly panting for breath on the crowded decks. The sailors had no room to execute the necessary work of the ship, and the officers of the ship were compelled to remonstrate with the officers of the men. The officers of the men, however; as many of them as were on board, suffered so much themselves, that they had a natural sympathy for their men, and therefore were unwilling to send them below. In these circumstances the deck was a scene of confusion—of noise—swearing—the crankling of ropes—the felling of blocks, and the mutual abuse of the men. The sailors, in order to effect by cunning what they could not do by direct force, contrived, as if unintentionally, to let the yard-arms and ropes swing so as to knock down our men by dozens.

Nothing is so unmanageable as a sailor, except by his own officer. They seem to regard us landsmen with contempt; and amongst the abuse which is dealt out from the mast-head by these porpoises, we are frequently saluted by the term of "Halloo, tailors! Below there!" and what is still worse, this is generally but the prelude to a block or rope dropped accidentally on our heads.

You have desired me to be minute; and as this is a scene to which you have not been accustomed, I have literally complied with your request. Indeed you can scarcely conceive, without having actually witnessed it, the hard, stubborn, jealous, mischievous nature of these sons of the ocean; they seem to have no satisfaction equal to that of playing us tricks, and certainly entertain a contempt for us, as if we were really tailors. One of our soldiers happened, unluckily, to ask if there were not some appearance of the wind rising. The sailor to whom the question was put, shook his head, and predicted a gale. The jest was immediately passed round; and even the captain and officers of the vessel joined in it so seriously as to alarm us all. They mischievously employed this pretence to clear the decks, and to rid themselves of the encumbrance of the men for the night. The officers alone were at liberty; but the seamen did not even deem it necessary to undeceive us.

I walked the deck the greater part of the night, and by some means or other escaped that horrible sea-sickness which my companions experienced. The coast of England was soon out of sight, and nothing was before us but an expanse of water. I could not but admire the silence of the officer who had the watch. I could not get a word from him; and he once or twice said to me with a sly leer "Be silent that I may hear the ship; this part of the sea is full of rocks; and if we were to go on during the night, and in such a fresh sea, we should all be lost."

This kind of hoaxing may serve you as a specimen of the sea-jests practised upon us. A military man should be sworn to the patient endurance of hardships, like the ancient knights; and it is not the least of these necessary hardships to have to serve with seamen. I should as soon expect a musket to swim, as expect a good understanding between seamen and soldiers.

Early on the following morning land was announced, and we all eagerly hurried on deck, that we might greet it with due welcome. Though I had not been twenty-four hours on the water, I had quite enough of it, and hailed the sight of land as an agreeable spectacle.

The Dutch coast was extremely low. When seen at a distance, the sea seems to overhang it. The tops of the trees are first seen, and the land appears as if it were rising from the bosom of the ocean. The water becomes shallower as we approach; and I have no doubt but that, in the course of ages, an industrious people like the Dutch, might recover some millions more acres from the bottom of the sea.

As we approached the land, we fell in with the ships of the division of Sir Richard Strachan, which, having preceded us in their departure, had arrived before us. Lord Chatham had embarked on board the *Venerable,* and was waiting the junction of the several divisions. In the meantime those inestimable sailors, the Deal boatmen, had been employed to take soundings, in order that we might enter some of the narrow channels, and escape the storm which we saw brewing in the north-east. Nothing indeed can be more perilous than these seas, every league of which has a rock or a flat; and if one of our vessels were to ground, our escape with life would be a miracle.

The Deal boatmen having made their report, and Sir Home Popham having confirmed their statement, Sir Richard Strachan ordered that the whole fleet should proceed into the Rompot.—Sir Home Popham led the way in the *Sabrina*; Sir Richard Keats followed. These operations took up the whole of the day of the 29th. On the following morning Sir Richard, being informed that Sir Richard Keats's division had made good its anchorage, issued orders that we, should all follow him. This was accordingly done; and after heaving through a very narrow channel, we all anchored in safety off the Veer-Gat.

You can scarcely be enabled to conceive by any description, however exact, the extreme difficulty and danger of this navigation, and the trepidation which we all felt for the safety of our ships. The manoeuvres were all executed in deep silence; and, from a sense of our common safety, the sailors and soldiers were for the moment in the most profound harmony. The sailors, however; seemed to feel their consequence, and the soldiers were compelled to submit: such are soldiers and sailors when acting together.

Orders were now given for us to land, and a scene of some confusion took place. The gun-boats well manned, pushed into the shore, and the enemy immediately abandoned a battery on our flank. I cannot account for their precipitate retreat, since the fort was certainly able to defend itself. To judge by the present evident preparations, we are not to expect any willing co-operation from the Dutch. But the Dutch, from some reason or other, seem to have lost their ancient character; whether it is that they are no longer fighting in a good cause, or from any other reason, I know not. I must correctly, however, inform you that their flotilla is commanded by one of the bravest men in Holland. Admiral De Winter will give us some trouble, or I am much mistaken. We shall not, however meet him as yet.

Upon the abandonment of the battery, our landing proceeded without further opposition. The enemy apparently did not like the shew which we made, and therefore left everything to our own way. Before nightfall we were all landed and immediately proceeded to take up our station. Our position is on the sand-hills called the Bree Sands. East Capelle is in front of us, and the fort of Der Haak, which the enemy have abandoned , on our flank.

The weather is bitter and rainy; but I understand that in this island such weather is very seasonable. That you may form a clear conception of our military operations, I have to add, that immediately on our landing, general Fraser was detached against Campveer. The town was summoned; but information has just been received that the Governor refuses to surrender till his fortifications be dismantled. He is a brave man, and stands, upon the point of honour; we must therefore humour him in his wishes, and preparations are making to bombard the town. It can scarcely hold out twenty-four hours.

Not being on this service, I have time to write to you. I am now in a very decent hut, and more comfortable than you would imagine. Orders are given not to unload our baggage till further progress shall be made in the expedition, by which is meant, till Flushing shall be taken, Middleburg, is to be summoned this night; I believe indeed it is done already.

You have frequently asked me how we soldiers live in camp. I can assure you very comfortably, or at least we have the art of making ourselves so. We enjoy ourselves like so many schoolboys. Three, four, or a dozen of us get into one tent, and pass the night as happy and as thoughtless as so many gipsies. It is true that we have some difficulty in mustering up a good supper; but wine is plentiful, and we have generally the luck to procure it good. As to a feather-bed, we have at present not one in camp; and our kitchen is as scantily furnished as our sitting-room. But we have so much to do, and so much to employ our thoughts and our imaginations, that these wants give us not a moment's uneasiness. The worst want is soap and water; it is very extraordinary that, amidst our abundant stock of other things, we should have forgotten the first article.

What should possess you with the notion that the Dutch would stretch out their arms to receive us? We have not seen an individual without arms in his hands. The French are all-powerful, and the Dutch must obey their master. Mynheer, moreover, does not seem pleased that we have come to give him the alternative of either submitting to us, or beating his town about his ears. I shrewdly suspect that he wishes us back again; be this as it may, no one comes near us.

Earl Chatham exhibits a spirit and energy worthy of his illustrious name. Is it not really a subject of regret, that the great talents of this nobleman should lose so much of their natural efficacy by his unhappy habits of indolence?

I am, my dear friend,
Yours &c

Letter 3

Campveer, August 2, 1809.
My Dear Friend,

You and the good people of England are much deceived if you have anticipated an easy accomplishment of the objects of our expedition. I think there cannot be a reasonable doubt but that we shall be enabled to effect them all; but I think it equally certain, from what I have already seen, and from the preparations going on around me, that there will be much hard fighting. The Dutch, with solitary exceptions, are at present against us; and, to do the French justice, they fight, like Trojans. There is another circumstance which much augments our difficulties; there is an incredible number of expatriated Irish, who have entered the French service, in this Island. These fellows fight against us with all the courage of their country, exasperated by desperation. You may expect, therefore, to hear that we shall sustain some loss before we reach Antwerp.

When I wrote to you last, General Fraser had been sent to summon Campveer. The commandant returned for answer, that it was his duty to maintain the town as long as he was enabled, and that, under this obligation, he should not be justified in surrendering it: this at least was the substance of his reply. Orders were immediately given from head-quarters to invest the town. The works were begun the same night, and the attack commenced in due form on the following morning. The garrison were as brisk on their side; and there was every appearance that they would hold out as long as one brick was upon another.

In the meantime, whilst the attack was proceeding on the land-side, the bombs and gun-vessels arrived before it in the Veer-Gat and Sir Home Popham directed an immediate bombardment which was carried into effect. The garrison received it bravely; and though the works were falling about their ears, they returned fire for fire. The effects of the bombardment, however, were tremendous. The report of the cannon was followed by the crash of houses, and bricks, mortar, and timber struck by the ball, were hurled over our heads into a distant part of the island; whole fragments of chimneys were in this manner driven over the town into the adjacent country. I never saw a cannonade so effectual; and I must do the brave garrison the justice to say that I never saw it better supported.

The falling lumber began at length to fill every space, and the fire of the garrison slackened, evidently because they had no room to work their guns. Night; now came on; and as it was evident that the town could not hold out much longer, the humanity of our commanders interposed, and the bombardment was slackened. The enemy, however, seemed to consider this forbearance as a reproach on their courage; and having cleared away some of the rubbish from their guns, recommenced their fire. In this manner, tempered only by the rain and darkness, the operations continued during a good part of the night.

In the morning the town presented a most melancholy spectacle of raids, Imagine a heavy circular mass of houses and walls battered by a cannonade of nearly fifty pieces of cannon, and this within three hundred yards of them, and you may form some idea of the horrible spectacle. The town really resembles nothing but a smoking pile of bricks. The fire seemed struggling for vent through the rubbish.

The garrison now offered to capitulate; and, much to the credit of our commanders, the offer was accepted, though the town was now most completely at their mercy. There was but one sentiment, however, in the British camp respecting these brave men, and that was an admiration of their courageous efforts. They fought as a British garrison would have fought under similar circumstances. The odds were too much against them, to leave them any chance of success; but they performed what is the duty of all soldiers under such circumstances—they defended their post to the utmost, and thereby delayed us, and gave time to their friends in other quarters.

The name of the commandant of this garrison is Lieutenant-Colonel Bogart; he is a brave man, and a most accomplished soldier. I am happy, for the sake of our cause, that he is not in Flushing; though, if we may believe report, the commandant of Flushing is an equally brave man. You know that I always speak fairly; and I have really no hesitation to say that, with the single exception of the English, the French soldiers and officers would bear the palm from the world. In external appearance, indeed, they are like so many vagabonds—ragged, dirty, and lean; but then they are all muscle and sinew: you may count their nerves like so many strings upon a fiddle. The officers, as many as I have seen of them, have the manners of gentlemen; and their old officers have an air of dignity and placid command, which impresses even an enemy with respect.

You will scarcely credit it, and yet it is but justice to mention it, that the French garrison which defended this small circuit of old walls, consisted only of four companies of infantry, and one of artillery—in all about four hundred men. We have given them good terms, and you will acknowledge that they have deserved it. They were allowed to march out with all the honours of war. You may be enabled to form some opinion by this, our first operation, what we are to expect, and of what stuff our enemy is made.

It is really glorious work to fight against the French; they give us sport enough to keep us warm. The Dutch seem to take the matter very deliberately; they do not certainly co-operate with us, and where they meet us, they fight with us. They seem, indeed, to have but one ruling principle—to take care of themselves. If they had to choose between England and France, they, would clearly decide for England; but as the present choice is between having their towns burned by the English, or defended by the French, I fear that they will adhere to the more immediate friend. The French have possession of their towns and houses.

You can form no conception of the ingenuity of the French, in the rapid construction, and even invention, of defensive works. They were clearly taken by surprise at the arrival of our expedition; yet so alert and ingenious were they, that before the town was invested, they had erected works of considerable strength, and even of magnitude. In this respect the French excel every people in the world. Their wonderful bridges over the Danube will outlive the bulletins which record them. When any difficulty occurs on their march, it is shortly made to give way to their ingenuity. We see hourly instances of this alertness of contrivance and execution. I do not say that the French did actually not expect us in Zealand; but they certainly did not know in what island we should land, nor what was the ultimate object of our expedition.

Upon entering into Campveer, the scene was melancholy to a degree. The bodies of women and children were lying dead in the streets. We were received with a kind of howl of distress, which spoke very forcibly to the heart. Much to the honour of our English soldiers, they seemed to feel for the distress which they had necessarily occasioned. Upon my word, war is a most horrible drama.

"You gentlemen of England,
"Who live at home at ease."—

can form no conception of it by the mere perusal of your *Gazettes*. If a cart or a coach be overthrown, and an unhappy individual therein break his leg, what a crowd collects around him in the streets of London, and how does every face wear the features of compassion and condolence! Now imagine these images infinitely multiplied. Imagine a space equal to St. James's Park, covered at every foot with wounded and dying men! some without their legs—some expiring in the most horrible agony; their eyes fixed upon the heavens, and their hearts, their imaginations reverting to their homes!—imagine all this, and you have some faint conception of a field of battle.

Campveer is the third town in rank of those in the Island of Walcheren. Whilst it stood, *i.e.* upon the first moment of our arrival, and before its bombardment, it was a lively, fresh-looking place; and though it stands low, is dry, and therefore not unhealthy. The houses are not so lofty as the books of travellers represent all Dutch towns; they are low, and cover a good space of ground. The Dutch seem to have the same ideas of comfort as the English in their country towns. Almost all the houses have porches before the gates, similar to what you have seen before the farmhouses in the North of England. To judge from first impressions, I should think that the inhabitants lived in a manner which even in England would be judged comfortable. Provisions were evidently in great plenty; and such enormous masses of dried fish, such piles of cheeses, that if the works had been stronger, the garrison would not have been starved out till doomsday.

Campveer is the celebrated smuggling depôt for the east coast of England. I have reason to believe that this trade existed to an incredible extent previous to our expedition. Neither Dutch nor English seem to have had any idea of obedience to the laws which restrained their commerce. Have you ever made the experiment of endeavouring to convince one of your Norfolk farmers that there was any immorality in smuggling? I have made this attempt frequently; but could never make them comprehend arguments so directly opposed to their interest.

You would naturally wish to know something of the climate of this island. It would not, perhaps, be fair to form any such precipitate conclusion as must necessarily result from speaking on it on an experience of only three days. To judge by our present specimen, it is the land of fogs and rain. Every half-hour we have a shower. I understand, however, that this weather is not considered as seasonable here, any more than in England. The summers are generally very dry, and the winters open and rainy. It is difficult, they say, to distinguish between spring and winter. From November to May is a continued and unbroken succession of rains and fogs. In the month of May the weather is insufferably cold, and the winds very violent. In June the weather becomes fine, but the heat is moderated by the sea. Upon the whole, the seasons, with the exception of the winter, seem to correspond with those in England. The winter alone is different—it is more open, that is to say, more rainy.

The general face of the island is flat; but there are some elevations which the people are pleased to call hills. I must confess, however, that the island has a very near resemblance to a billiard-table; so level, that a ball rolled from one side, would pass without impediment to the other. I will not, however, enter into a detailed account of the island at present; for, to confess the truth, I know too little of it. If all travellers would be equally candid, there would not be so many useless volumes.

I am afraid we are about to suffer a most dreadful inconvenience. To explain this to you, it may be necessary to describe the situation of this island. The Island of Walcheren, like almost all the Islands of Zealand, has certainly, in former times, been at the bottom of the sea; but the industry of man, which, under certain impulses, is to be daunted by nothing, attempted to push the sea back, and succeeded in the daring effort. Dikes were accordingly erected, and an island was thus scooped out, and fenced off from the bed of the ocean. The Island of Walcheren, therefore, has no imperfect resemblance to a round basin, or a deep soup-plate, floating in the sea. Now, imagine that the side of this basin, or plate, if broken down, so as to render the body of it level with the sea, and you have an idea of the peril and inconvenience to which I am alluding.

The Flushingers, as we have learned, are about to cut the dikes, and to admit the sea. If they should really execute this purpose, and the weather should be tempestuous, so as to bring the waves up to the dikes, and should continue so for any length of time. Heaven knows what will become of us! It is true that this measure would be attended with the certain ruin of the island; but the French are the masters of it, and the Dutch proprietors only would suffer. It is a military maxim to hope for the best; and therefore I will dismiss these apprehensions.

The enemy have evacuated Middleburg, the town being open, and by no means tenable. The grand stand is to be made off Flushing, against which we are to advance without delay. There are two or three batteries, however, which must be previously disposed of. If report may be credited the garrison of Flushing is very strong; and what is worse, we are under great apprehensions that it will be rendered still stronger. The navigation is so difficult, and the forts for the present are so strong, . that our gun-boats cannot get round so as to cut off the communication between Flanders and the island.

Yesterday, according to the flying reports of the island, a large party were landed from Cadsand, and we have reason to believe that a much stronger corps is advancing from Ghent. To say all in a word, our operations begin to assume a serious appearance, and there is something like business going forwards. We should think all this but matter of insignificance if the weather were but favourable; but unluckily everything is against us. The ancient Dutch must have had no inconsiderable portion of courage, to have fixed upon this island for their habitation; it is truly a land of water.

There are a number of Scotch families settled in this island, some of them in the towns, and some of them in the farm-houses.

I made this discovery this morning when I was addressed in Scotch by an inhabitant. These people, very honourably to themselves, observe a strict neutrality. They will not fight against us, and they consider it as treachery to co-operate with us. I do not know what our commander in chief will finally determine against the native British subjects; but if I may judge from the general tone of the higher officers, they will be left to pursue their own line of conduct. We all take much interest in them.

Two or three of us have been to Middleburg, where the head-quarters are now established. My division is for the present at Campveer, where we have to hold guard over smoking ruins. This morning, however, I rose early, and, accompanied by two or three other officers, walked to Middleburg. The road is a very good one, and the scenery not unpleasant. The distance between Campveer and Middleburg is four miles, and the road is much frequented. The Dutch inhabitants of Middleburg seemed perfectly at their ease; carts were going along the road, and no one would have judged that an enemy was in the country.

As soon as we shall have driven the French from the island, the Dutch inhabitants will be heartily our friends. At present their subjugation is so complete, that the utmost to be expected from them is neutrality. The French, upon their part, seem to have neither confidence nor opinion of them; they take all the brunt of fighting upon themselves, and satisfy themselves with raising forced contributions upon Mynheer, as if for his own defence. The weather at this instant is very fine; the sun shines, and everything looks verdant and delightful.

The verdure of this island is not to be exceeded even in England. The grass and corn are luxuriant to a degree. The harvest I should suppose is much more backward here than in England; but if I may judge, by the apparent burthen of the land, the produce here is superior to what it is in England. The stalks seem insufficient to support the ears.

A very brave action has already taken place at the gates of Flushing. The 14th and 81st Regiments followed the garrison of Middleburg to the very walls of Flushing, and endeavoured to force an entry with them by a direct assault. It is generally reported in the army that they would have succeeded, had it not been deemed advisable to call them off. The garrison of Flushing were panic-struck at the daring attempt. It is indeed impossible by any words to do justice to the courage and spirit of our troops.

Our loss at Campveer, and in the skirmishes during yesterday and the preceding day, has been very inconsiderable. I should suppose, on a rough calculation, about eighty men and officers were killed, and about twice the number wounded. Almost the whole of these were killed and wounded at Campveer. That little garrison defended itself manfully. If the works had been stronger, we should have found this town very troublesome. There is a report here, but I know not whence it comes, that General Bernadotte is at Antwerp, that the French have thirty thousand men at Lillo, and seventy thousand at Bergen-op-Zoom, This latter fortress is not, I believe, within the line of our operations. If it should be, we shall have enough to do; for it is the strongest fortress in the Provinces. Antwerp is not strong in itself; but the works in its neighbourhood are formidable.

Our commander in chief exceeds all our expectations. There cannot be a doubt, I think, of the final success of our expedition; and if it should so succeed, England will at least be indebted to us for having freed her from the possibility of invasion for a century to come. The efforts which the French have been making to create a marine force behind the Islands of the Scheldt, are truly extraordinary; the forests are at hand, and the banks of the river are almost covered with docks. If this work had continued much longer, we should have found a fleet at sea, without knowing whence it came; and this fleet, moreover, would have been a Dutch fleet, which I take to be totally another kind of thing to a French fleet. It was clearly the intention of Bonaparte to have secretly created a fleet whilst he was fighting his battles on the Continent; and after he had finished the work of conquest there, to have made some attempt on us by way of Holland.

It is for this reason only that these Provinces have not as yet been subjected to the conscription, Bonaparte, who has sagacity enough to knew, the value of men, has learned that the Dutch are better sailors than the French: his plan, therefore, is to reduce the Dutch to a naval conscription, and to fight his sea battles by means of these Hollanders. I have no doubt but that an English fleet would give a very good account of a Dutch one; but of this I am certain, that a Dutch fleet would be more troublesome than a French one. Our Government, therefore, and ourselves, will have deserved well, if we destroy this plan in its cradle. Farewell! I shall write daily, and send the letters as often as opportunity shall serve.

Yours &c. &c.

Letter 4

Middleburg, August 5, 1809.

My Dear Friend,

Since my last letter (I know not when this will reach you) we, have been very busy: the enemy keep us in warm employment, and, to say the truth, both parties seem equally determined. The military laws of France are very severe. If a commander surrender a town or fort before an absolute and evident necessity, he has to expect no mercy. General Monnet seems totally a different kind of man to General Bruce. The latter has given to Sir John Hope a quiet possession of the Bevelands. I really think that he might have stood a few shot for the honour of his name.

Immediately after the surrender of Campveer, orders were issued to march for Flushing. It will be necessary to besiege this town in due form. The works are very strong, and upwards of a mile in circuit. It is well for us that we are attended by a naval force, or we might lay long enough by the land side of it. On the sea front it is not exposed; because, from the construction of its fortifications, it was less apprehensive of danger. No one, I believe, ever foresaw the extraordinary predominance of the British navy. Have no fear of us at home; for wherever your ships can reach, nothing can withstand you. Imagine a battery of one or two hundred guns playing upon a small given space, and tell me what can withstand it. Flushing, Fort Lillo, and Antwerp must surrender to its after a few days' bombardment. Our armies have little to do but to confine the enemy within their walls.

The enemy did. not suffer us to form our investment without a vigorous opposition. General Graham had some warm work with them. A party of them, which were posted on the Middleburg road, were very troublesome; but General Houston attacked them vigorously, and they fled before him like so many frighted sparrows. Every attack proves one circumstance which is very strongly in our favour—the trench cannot stand the onset of the British troops.

When a French party see an English party of equal strength to themselves, they immediately look found them for some advantage ground; they then draw themselves up, in which they exceed any soldiers in the world. The British in the meantime rush forwards. The French, waiting with the utmost deliberation till the British get within the distance most effectual for their fire, discharge their pieces; the two first ranks then kneel, and the second and third fire, and so on during the whole depth of the column. The French never think of retreating till they all give one discharge; and from their deliberation, an effect of their discipline and habit, they generally make dreadful execution. By this time the British have reached them; they then fly, and endeavour to form again. If they succeed, which they almost always do once or twice, they again receive us in the same manner. You will understand from this brief description, why our loss in wounded is sometimes so serious.

That you may now be enabled to form a tolerably correct judgement of our future operations, I will state to you the present disposition of our army before Flushing. Major-General Graham commands on the right: this division consists of three brigades; the 2nd Brigade under General Graham; the 3rd under General Ackland, and the 7th under General Leith.

The centre is under Generals Houston and Stewart, and consists of two brigades, the 8th and the 12th.

The left is under Major-Generals Picton and Brigadier-General Rotenburg, and consists of the 13th and 11th Brigades.

There are three battalions, moreover, left to garrison Middleburg, and one at Campveer. I am at the former of these places, but go daily, and almost hourly, to the siege.

What I stated to you in my last, respecting the Irish brigade, has been verified. They are very strong and numerous in the garrison of Flushing; and the apparent resolution of the commandant is attributed to them. It is my sincere wish, however, that these fellows may effect their escape; for if they fall into our hands, we shall be compelled; I am afraid, to deliver them over to the law. But, considering the hardships, which they have suffered, that they were actually drawn from their country, and compelled to enter into some service for subsistence though we do not forgive them, yet we all pity therm. There is but one wish in the army in this respect; and from what I see of our excellent commander in chief, I am persuaded that he would have no satisfaction in having some hundreds. of these poor creatures hung up under the sentence of the law.

There are many deserters join us daily; they are chiefly Spaniards, the remnants of the army of Romana, who, had it not in their power to effect their escape with their brave countrymen. They are of course very discontented with their treatment under the French Government: since the escape of Romana, they have all been confined to garrison duty, and were sent hither, as being out of the way. We learn by these that the garrison of Flushing are resolved to hold put to the last; but that the town is not in a condition to support a bombardment by sea. This, in fact, is our main hope. If it were not for our navy, Flushing might hold out for six weeks. I believe I have before informed you that Flushing is situated very low, and that apparently it is the most unhealthy town in this half-drowned island.

Even the inhabitants of Middleburg, though distant only five miles, speak with horror of Flushing. They have a kind of proverb in the island, that no one can live in Flushing but a sailor. When a fog hangs over the town, it presents a spectacle of desolation. If an English garrison should hereafter be stationed here, the surgeon will have enough business on his hands.

The late bombardment of Campveer was more destructive than we had imagined. Many of the townspeople were destroyed by it, and amongst them some domesticated Englishmen, who, having made their fortunes, I suppose by smuggling, had fixed in this town. It is incredible the number there are of these English, Irish, and Scotch refugees. They have doubtless been tempted to settle here from the comparative cheapness of provisions. which are not one-half the price that they bear in England. Our arrival, however, has much altered, for the present, at least, this moderate price.

We have but this instant received intelligence of the surrender of Fort Rammekins, a most important piece of service, as it enables the fleet to come round into the West Scheldt, and thereby not only to take Flushing on its sea flanks, but to cut off all communication between Cadsand and Walcheren. The enemy are very powerful in Cadsand; and in a Council of War which has been held on the occasion, it has been deemed advisable not to venture any operations in that quarter.

You can scarcely form any adequate idea of the gallantry of our seamen, even when employed on the land-service. The island of Walcheren, as I have before mentioned, is very thickly wooded with a stunted timber, resembling bushes. The French, from their superior knowledge of the place, have availed themselves of this advantage; and the few men which we have as yet lost, have been shot by their marksmen, planted for the occasion behind these bushes. It had even become dangerous to pass anything in the shape of a tree. The seamen of the gun-brigs, of their own free-will, undertook the service of clearing these, bushes, and have performed it so effectually, that the Frenchmen are now quiet.

Our brave Tars made a sport of this dangerous service. Their only reward has been the spoil which they have taken; and there are few of them but have a rifle-gun, a dirk; or some other article of a similar kind, to produce as a proof of their courage and success. I must not forget to mention, by the way, that the French sharp-shooters infinitely exceed our own, and that they seem to set more value on them.

Sir John Hope, we understand, has effected the complete conquest of South Beveland. This island was commanded by General Bruce, a Scotchman, who, deeming it indefensible, has withdrawn all his garrison into Bergen-op-Zoom, by the Antwerp road. Everyone here seems to consider this general not to have done his duty; and you may imagine that the Scotsmen are peculiarly indignant with him. Whence is it that the Scotsmen in foreign service do not maintain the reputation of their country?—It is that they want the impulse of a good cause.

As to the French fleet, by all accounts, they exceed fourteen sail of the line, besides frigates. I am very sorry to have to inform you that they have all effected their escape down the Scheldt; and I have still more regret in adding, that it is the general opinion of the army, that they will ultimately escape us. The river is navigable to Antwerp; but the navigation is so dangerous, that though they may venture, we must not. Every mile of the river, on both sides, is planted with forts. You will understand, from these circumstances, that we have nothing to expect unless we can take Antwerp, From Flushing to the Flemish side, the Scheldt is so broad, that you scarcely can see the opposite side; but from Sanvliet to Antwerp, the Scheldt is not broader than the Thames.

As far as we can at present understand, the projected plan of operations is as follows:—After Flushing is taken, Lord Chatham will assemble the land-force at Bathz, in South Beveland, and then pass over to the east bank of the eastern branch, of the Scheldt. He is then to continue along that line till he reaches the body of the river. Sir Richard Strachan is in the meantime to proceed down the river, and to clear the channel. In this manner the combined forces are to advance to Lillo, where they expect some work.

I have already given you a brief idea of the nature of the dikes. I have since been, informed that the country has been flooded between Lillo and Antwerp; and this intelligence has excited some unpleasant anticipations in the army. It was before believed that the French would not thus entirely destroy the country; but should it not have been remembered that it was not their own country which they were thus flooding, and that they are not the kind of people to have any feelings of reluctance in providing for their own defence by the ruin of others

There could not possibly have been a more able piece of service than the landing of the troops, and the passage through the Veer-Gat, It is the general subject of praise throughout the army. Had it not been for this skilful operation, the army would not have been landed even by this time; for the wind has been in the wrong point. A more material advantage, however is, that it has had the effect of saving many valuable lives. The difficulty of the passage of the Veer-Gat was so great, that the enemy had no idea that we should make any attempt in that quarter: the consequence was, that they were totally unprepared to oppose our landing, Under these circumstances we made it good without loss or opposition.

The character of the commander in chief rises daily and hourly in the opinion of the men. He possesses one most valuable quality—a regard for the lives of his men. Before he requires a dangerous piece of service, he invariably considers its probable cost; and if the expense be but the life of two or three men, he weighs the matter well before he commands it. You may readily imagine that this feature renders him popular. Every soldier and officer, I presume, is willing to expose his life in a regular and professional way; but no one, with any portion of common sense, can forgive the man who uselessly forces him into the cannon's mouth. I have to make an observation which may appear invidious, but is nevertheless but too true.

It is, that, from several instances which have fallen within my own experience, I have been led to conclude that the naval officers have less of this considerate humanity than those of the army. How many valuable lives are daily lost by improvident attempts to cut out mercantile vessels under an enemy's fort! Were I the commander of a ship of war, I would never expose my men against such pitiful advantages. The public gain has no proportion to the public loss. You will pardon, me for an observation which may appear to you to partake something of the standing and immortal jealousy of the army and of the navy.

The weather in this country is infinitely more variable than in England. We are so completely surrounded by water, that every wind that blows, must bring us rain. A dry month would be a miracle here. This, however, has its advantage; the island is as green and as bright as an emerald, the grass luxuriant, and the corn heavy.

I am, my dear Sir,
Yours &c.

Letter 5

Lines before Flushing, Aug. 9, 1809.
My Dear Sir,
Since I wrote to you last, we have done very little. The garrison of Flushing seem resolved to give us as much trouble as possible. General Monnet has certainly received positive instructions to hold out as long as possible, in order that he may give time for the assembling of the French army at Antwerp. Everything seems in a bustle. In the meantime, we, upon our part, are ceaselessly employed in bringing the, artillery from the ships; and we have, already raised some very considerable works.

The weather, however, is dismally bad, and the enemy annoy us by their incessant fire. Whilst our men are at work, a soldier is constantly employed to watch the flashes of the town guns. As soon as he sees a flash, he gives the word, and the workmen all fall prostrate. You can scarcely imagine how effectual this method has been. It necessarily, however, delays the workmen.

The number of our army now before Flushing exceeds

15,000 men, under the command of Sir Eyre Coote. In the whole Island of Walcheren we have about 18,000; the 26th Regiment remains to garrison Middleburg, and there is a battalion at Campveer. With the exception of these deductions, the whole of our army in Walcheren is before Flushing. Our lines are in a semicircle, extending from the north-west to the south-east of the town. We have but just completed the trenches, and two six-gun batteries are ready to come into immediate play. Nothing, however, can be done till the ships come round; and the wind has as yet been unfavourable. Lord William Stewart is to lead this division; and there is a confident hope that the town, bombarded by sea and land must surrender within twenty-four hours.

The day before yesterday we had very warm work; the garrison made a sally, to the number of 2000 men. They drew up very manfully, and formed under the walls. Their object was to dislodge the advanced party of General Graham's brigade. This advanced party might consist of about 600 men. The enemy advanced to the attack with a great shew of resolution. The French officers are scarcely inferior to our own; they pointed out the line of march with their swords, and themselves led the way.

Their charge was warm; but the deliberate courage of the English repelled it. The third battalion of the Royals, and the 5th and 35th Regiments bore the main brunt. The 95th Regiment, and some detachments from the German Legion, shared in the peril and the honour. After a very sharp contest, the enemy were repelled, and compelled to retreat to their walls in some confusion. They have not as yet ventured out. This attack continued in all about two hours; it commenced at four in the afternoon, and about seven everything was over.

Upon the first alarm, the whole army was in motion; but our brave fellows terminated the business before the action became general. They seemed indeed to fear lest they should lose: the honour of obtaining the victory by themselves. It is but justice, however, to add, that nothing could evince better, discipline than the advance of the French troops; they marched towards us as if on a parade. The British, upon their part, allowed them to come within musket-shot, when they poured upon them such a cool and deliberate fire, as immediately threw them into some confusion. Our men then leaped from the trenches, and charged the enemy with bayonets.

The French made many fruitless efforts to keep their ground, and after they were broken, to form again; but the English repeatedly attacked them. The battle continued, as I have said, nearly two hours, at the end of which time the enemy were completely routed. The French officers again and again endeavoured to rally them. These officers merit all the fame which they have acquired. They have but one blot on the military, character—they are cruel to an extreme degree. But no one who has ever been opposed to them must say a word against their courage. They fight like heroes; and if the men were but equal to their leaders, they would be invincible,

As to our operations in other quarters, the *Gazettes* will probably inform you that Sir John Hope is in Beveland with about 20,000 men. General the Marquis of Huntley, and Lord Rosslyn, are to join him this day; Sir John will thus have a force of nearly 30,000 men, and in Walcheren we shall still have nearly 18,000. Sir Richard Strachan is gone to Bathz, which has been attacked by the enemy. Some of our gun-boats, under Sir Home Popham, have already gone up the river. This is all the intelligence I can give you for the present. Flushing seems resolved to hold out, and the enemy are evidently collecting on the banks of the Scheldt. I still, however, hope that all will go well. Our force is great, and the enemy dare not front us.

Our army, as you may suppose, is very unpleasantly lodged. They have built themselves huts; but the rain penetrates them, and nothing can be more comfortless. We look to the fall of Flushing for better accommodation. There are positive orders against landing more than a certain weight of baggage. Many of the soldiers are without blankets, and there is scarcely a change of linen throughout the army.

The King of Holland has been in our neighbourhood. I wish

he would be pleased to venture a little nearer us; his Majesty might have a chance of a visit to England. Everything is at present at a stand till Flushing surrenders. I have been employing myself in drawing up an account of the island, which I can assure you is a most delightful spot; so thickly inhabited, the houses so clean and comfortable, and everything cheap and plentiful. As I have nothing, for the present, more to add of our military operations, I will throw together all the information I have gathered of the island, and of the province to which it belongs. You would give me more thanks for this if you knew the trouble it has cost me.

Perhaps there are few provinces in the European part of the world which are less known than Zealand, and the several islands which compose it. This ignorance is not to be excused by any absence of value or importance in the object. In all ages of the world, Holland has performed its part on the public theatre; and where Holland has been called into action, the grand component part of her strength, the Province of Zealand, has never been behind hand. In the Spanish wars, the Zealanders fought with a perseverance and fury which much forwarded the main cause; and in every subsequent contest for liberty, or for supposed liberty, the Zealanders have always taken the lead.

It might be imagined that such a province, and such a people, might not be so perfectly buried in obscurity as to remain unknown to their European neighbours; but it sometimes happens to nations as to individuals, that merit, and even actual importance and solid worth, are not the invariable passports, to distinction. A petty German Prince, by the bustle which he will contrive to create around him, will intrigue himself into consequence and celebrity; and Strelitz or Wolfenbuttle will be known, where Zealand has been passed over.

The Province of Zealand, moreover, in a geographical point of view, is not very favourably situated. It is composed of a number of islands which are situated at the mouth of the Scheldt, where that river opens into the sea. It even takes its name, Zealand, or Sea-Land, from this circumstance of its position. Being on the immediate strand of the sea, and as it were a continuation of it, it lies much lower than any part of the United Provinces; and, according to the most accurate observation, the sea daily becomes more shallow in its vicinity. The distance between Walcheren and Flanders is very considerable, so much so, that Cadsand is scarcely perceptible, except in a clear day; yet from the decreasing depth of the water, the Zealanders anticipate the speedy union of their several islands with the mainland, and with each other.

It must not be forgotten, however, that in the high tides, and more particularly where the wind concurs with these tides, the sea rolls forward in most tremendous magnitude, and threatens to bury the inhabitants and their defensive works in one grave. Nothing, indeed, can be more horrible than the appearance of one of these islands in a tempest of this description. The dreadful mass of accumulated waters, wave impelling wave, seems to be curling over them; the islands sink, in a word, beneath the level of the waters, and a ship on their immediate coast, only sees the summit of the steeples, as the waves momentarily sink. It really seems a miracle how they have been so long preserved; and when we read in their annals of the dreadful ravages which they have occasionally suffered under these winds and graves, it is impossible not to shudder with apprehension. None but a Dutchman, a man accustomed to the sea from his birth, could possibly endure such an habitation.

The islands of Zealand are chiefly formed by the branches of the Scheldt. The line of the Scheldt, from its mouth to Antwerp; is about fifty miles, during the greater part of which distance it much exceeds the width of the Thames, and, to confess the truth, is a much grander river. The banks, on both sides, are very strongly fortified, in the first instance by the Spaniards, and recently by the French and Dutch.

These forts are about two miles from each other, and are so artificially placed, as to command the channel of the river through every mile of its course, the forts on the east bank being two miles distant, whilst the forts on the west bank, are so situated as to be halfway between the forts on the opposite side.

In this manner is the line of this river secured against any foreign attack. The Dutch, however, have another, and perhaps a better security in their dikes, upon cutting of which they can so flood their country, as to preclude the possibility of any attack by land. The only chance of an enemy, under these circumstances, is when the tides are unusually low, and their force so commanding, as to give no time for the operation of this defence. Under these circumstances, if they can anticipate the flowing of the waters, the country, strong as it is by nature and art, may be entered, and perhaps subdued. But if the Dutch have time to cut their dikes, and about ten days for the waters to follow, they are invincible.

From Antwerp to Fort Sanvliet, a distance of fifteen miles, the river Scheldt flows in one undivided stream, about as broad as the Thames at Battersea, but twice or three times its depth, so as to be navigable by the largest vessels. At Sanvliet the Island of South Beveland interposes, as it were, in the bed of the river, and thus divides it into two streams, of which the one is called the West Scheldt, and the other the East Scheldt.

These two branches, circling round the Island of Beveland, extend themselves in a wide fork when they reach its northern extremity, and in this fork, in this interval between the Eastern and Western Scheldt, are situated the several Islands of Cadsand, Walcheren, North Beveland, and Wolversdyck,; and on the eastern branch, of the Scheldt, those of Schowen and Duyveland. These several islands, of which Walcheren and South Beveland are the most important, fill up that portion of the sea into which the Scheldt opens itself, and which is therefore usually termed the Mouth of the Scheldt. The channels between these islands will be severally described when I come to speak of the topography of the Province.

These islands, with St. Philip's Land, and the Islet of Ter Tholen, constitute the Province of Zealand, —a province of which it may well be said, that one-half of it is always under water. They are all situated in that. fork of the river which is created by the interposition of the Island of South Beveland in the main bed of the stream, and by the subsequent extension of them after they have reached the northern extremity of that island.

It is evident, from this mere description of the situation of these islands, that they constitute a place of refuge peculiarly favourable for an enemy; the navigation is so dangerous, and the channels are so narrow, that it has been deemed impossible for any hostile force to penetrate behind the islands at the mouth of the Scheldt. Under this persuasion, the French have availed themselves of its local advantages to shelter such part of their flotilla as, by escaping along the shallows of the Dutch coast, have been enabled to elude our cruisers.

The country of the Scheldt, moreover, is very thickly wooded. This vicinity of the forest, and the perfect and uninterrupted tranquillity of the workmen, have encouraged the French to attempt the creation of a navy in the docks of Antwerp and its vicinity; they have already done much, and. from the continuance of the same causes, more is to be expected of them. The resources of France, and the fortune of France, are unhappily in the hands of a man whose ambition is forwarded by his talents, and who, thus assisted and impelled, has exalted the French power to a most dangerous point of predominance. Europe must not long rest upon her arms.

It is not very easy to convey to a foreigner an adequate idea of the face of the country. From what has been already said, it might be imagined that it was wet, marshy, and scarcely habitable. This, however, is by no means the case. Though the land be low, it is dry, and not unhealthy. This may be imputed to the numerous dikes, canals, and intersections which drain off the water. The Dutch, notoriously the most industrious of all the nations in the world, have very naturally applied this industry to the remedy or alleviation of their own immediate inconveniences; and accordingly every island in Zealand exhibits the pleasing spectacle of the effects of industry, even in opposition to Nature.

One thing is certain, that, in despite of every apparent source of sickness, such a thing as ill health is scarcely known amongst these hardy islanders. When an Englishman beholds these islands from the sea, his first idea is, that it must be impossible for the inhabitants to retain their health on such an abode. He is afterwards, however, compelled to yield to experience, and to acknowledge that England is not the only habitable country on the face of the globe.

Neither is the surface of these islands such a complete level as, they have been described. In Walcheren in particular, there are some considerable elevations, which, though not perhaps actually hills, are still greatly above the surface of the sea. When the other islanders speak of Walcheren, they must term it an hilly region.

The climate of all the islands of Zealand is certainly not very favourable. From the quantity of water which surrounds them, it is scarcely possible for them to have a week without rain. From this very circumstance, however, their winters are much milder than those of England. It may even be a question whether the maritime counties of England are not equally subject to damps and rains. Ireland has nearly double the quantity of annual rain to what falls in England; yet no one has ever considered Ireland as an unpleasant climate. It is certain that the Islands of Zealand are not more subject to rain than Ireland; and however open the season may be, it seldom happens that the harvest is spoiled by it. This cannot be said of the climate of Ireland.

As to produce, the islands of Zealand produce everything which is necessary either to the comfort or enjoyment of life; and from the moisture of the climate, and the fertility of the soil, this produce is as abundant as it is various. The meadows are infinitely more verdant and more luxuriant than in England. It seldom, perhaps never, has happened that, from the drought of the season, the cattle are starving for the want of herbage; a spectacle not uncommon in the midland counties of more southern kingdoms. In the luxuriant grass of the islands of Zealand the cattle attain an immense size, and might be still larger, and nearer perfection, if the inhabitants gave any attention to the breed: but agriculture is in its first stage throughout all the provinces of Holland. Every man follows in the track which his father has marked out before him; and innovation would be considered as tantamount to voluntary ruin.

The first step to improvement is to examine the grounds of the established practice. From this extraordinary abundance of all natural produce, every article of life is, at least, one-half less than what it costs in England. Fish of every species are in great plenty. In the winter season, the islands are periodically visited by wild fowl of every kind. The plenty of a Zealand farmhouse very nearly resembles that of an old Yorkshire hall. The racks groan beneath the piled bacon; half the rooms in the house are filled with cheeses; the liquors are ten or a dozen years old; the orchards are loaded with fruit; and the homestead crowded with cattle. Such is the scene which almost every house presents. A Dutchman never deems himself to be secure against famine till he has laid in enough to stand a siege.

Amongst the other natural produce of this island, the wheat is well known to the agriculturists of Europe. It is an hardy and heavy species; it stands all weathers, and is particularly productive in the grinding ; it is known by the name of the Zealand Wheat; and as its hardness secures the island from the uncertainty of the, seasons, so does its proportionate productiveness render it always comparatively cheap. The same may be asserted as to the pasturage. So many cattle, and particularly sheep, are raised and fed in the rich meadows of Walcheren, Beveland, and the other islands, that meat of all kinds is in great plenty, and, as compared with the prices in England, most extraordinarily cheap.

Nothing indeed is scarce in these islands but fuel. Most of the islands have very respectable groves, avenues, and even some woods: but as these have not been raised without the most extreme difficulty, and the most assiduous care, the Dutch will not suffer them to be used as fuel. The common fuel of the islands, therefore, is turf, or coal, which is brought from Germany; and from the heavy price of cartage to the water, and freightage over; these are both very dear. If Walcheren should be incorporated in the British Empire, it might be very cheaply supplied from

Newcastle or Sunderland.

The island of Walcheren, as has been before observed, is not unhealthy, except to foreign visitors, before they have been accustomed to the climate. The numerous canals and water intersections serve as so many drains, by which the soil is kept dry, so that there are but few marshes, though the ground be so extremely low. The other islands of Zealand, and even some parts of Walcheren, are not free from disease; the most usual are agues and intermittent fevers, which generally attend the rainy season. These fevers, however, though very troublesome, and sometimes very lingering, are never dangerous; they have not the same putridity as what is termed in England the Kentish Fever, though they very much resemble it.

The medical treatment is in both the same; and there can be no reason to doubt but that proper precautions, upon the first appearance of the autumnal rains, would entirely prevent the complaint; and it is certain that, with the single exception of Flushing, the inhabitants of Walcheren and the Bevelands are long livers, and have that external appearance of health and solid strength, which never characterises the inhabitants of unwholesome climates. The occasional sharpness of the weather, and the frequent winds, tend much to purify the air, and to diminish the effect and malignity of those putrid exhalations, which in all humid climates are more or less fatal to animal life.

It should not be here forgotten to recommend to the visitant of Zealand, that he should imitate the modes of life which he will see in practice around him, and that whilst in Zealand, he should live as the Zealanders live. The careless confidence of the South of Europe, as far as regards health, will not do here. He must go warmly clothed, and his clothes must be of a quality which are weather-proof. How many painful and lingering diseases might be avoided by attention to the precepts of Dr. Cheyne:—the feet dry, the head cool, and the stomach externally warm. It is an invariable practice in Zealand to be wrapped up next to the skin in an envelope of flannel. This vestment is put on in November, and in June is gradually removed, by daily cutting off a larger or smaller piece. Under this protection the Zealander defies all weathers, and in the most humid climate of the world, scarcely knows what sickness is. Half the diseases in life originate in the confidence of health. With due precautions, there, would be little occasion for the frequent application to physicians.

"God never made his work for man to mend."

Man is made like other animals, with whatever is necessary to the due maintenance of his system; he is sufficient for himself in body and in mind. If his machine fail in his destined round, it is his own fault.

The Zealanders, moreover, have another remedy against the effects of their climate. This is the use of tobacco. They are the greatest smokers in the universe. A stranger unaccustomed to tobacco, cannot so easily reconcile himself to this their national habit, as to their general use of flannel; but if he value the permanence of his health, he will endeavour even to accommodate himself to this. It is a necessary defence against the climate; it certainly prevents cold, and most probably braces the system. It is certainly, not necessary to carry it to the extreme in which it is used by the Dutch. Strangers should adopt it as one of the established medicines against the climate. If they convert it into an enjoyment, an excuse for indolence, and perfect immobility, they become true Dutchmen. The moderate use of tobacco is an humid climate is most certainly salutary, if not necessary.

The prevailing winds in most of the islands are the westerly in summer, and the cast and north-east in winter. The westerly winds, which generally continue nearly the whole of the summer, are necessarily fraught with rains; and accordingly the natural .summer of Zealand resembles the May of England, in which, there is an almost hourly transition from rain to sunshine. This weather, moreover, is considered by physicians as peculiarly productive of gouts, rheums, and scurvies.

Accordingly, in some of these islands, these several complaints are very predominant. The scurvy most probably belongs naturally to every maritime situation. If this disease were correctly defined, it might perhaps be termed a disease originating in the predominance of a salt humour. Gouts and coughs may be prevented or remedied by attention to what has been said, above. In some of the fenny parts, bordering upon what is called the Drowned Land, where the mud during the ebb emits putrid effluvia, and wholesome water is scarce; the inhabitants are afflicted with continual retching, and other appendages of putrid infection. The use of bark, however, almost immediately removes these alarming symptoms, and the system apparently only suffers for the time.

There is another disease which is not easily accounted for; all the inhabitants, of whatever age, are almost devoured by worms. In the other kingdoms of Europe, children are frequently afflicted with this troublesome complaint; but it very rarely extends to mature age. In Zealand, on the other hand, man, woman, and child suffer most cruelly under this disease in all its degrees. The inhabitants, in their medical management of this complaint, are contented with purgatives; a remedy which they must sometimes find worse than the evil which it is intended to cure. The folly of the last age was bleeding; the folly of the present is the frequent, the immoderate, the dangerous use of purgatives.

There cannot be a doubt but that in some former century, the whole of the Province of Zealand was at the bottom of the sea, and that it has been recovered thence only by the united industry of man, and the general retreat of the waters, This retreat, however, has been so gradual, and so uncertain, that even in the recollection of many now living tempests and tides have occurred, in which the sea has nearly half over-flooded an island, and threatened the whole Province with submersion. On the following day, indeed, the sea returns to its ancient bed; and there remains perhaps for about thirty or forty years, when it again, as it were, comes forward to put in its claim, and to mark out its dominion. The inhabitants, however, having escaped the first visitation, forget it before the return of the second; and thus, like the inhabitants in the neighbourhood of Ætna or Vesuvius, live tranquil and contented, though in hourly danger of extermination.

From this account of the original formation of the soil, it will not be expected that any of the islands, have any minerals which are worthy of being mentioned. The soil has still the appearance of what has been deposited by the sea; it is impossible to mistake its origin or composition. The time may perhaps. arrive when the natural history of Zealand may be subjected to more accurate investigation. At present the materials are so insufficient, that it would have the appearance of pedantry to run through all the technical, divisions. The above, is the most ample account which I can give.

Yours &c.

Letter 6

Lines before Flushing, August 11, 1809.

My Dear Friend,

Everything seems so perfectly at a stand since I last wrote that we resemble rather a camp on Coxheath, than a besieging force. Everything on our part is preparation; the enemy are still brisk, but since the last repulse they have not ventured at a sortie. The English soldiers are as indisputably superior to the French in the charge by the bayonet, as the French soldiers are superior to the English in standing fire. The moment our Englishmen receive the enemy's fire, they rush in upon them, and nothing can restrain them. The French knowing that such is their custom sometimes avail themselves of it, and purposely give way in which case our brave fellows usually rush upon the very mouths of their artillery, and the slaughter is dreadful.

There is one remarkable difference between the French and English in the attack by the bayonet. The English muskets are all of the same length; the bayonet charge, therefore, is in one line, and as it were with one momentum. On the other hand, the French soldiers have muskets of all sorts and sizes, the older soldiers having the full length musket, the boys and younger men muskets of a length and weight suited to their strength.

This produces a prodigious difference in the charges of the two armies. In some respects, however, this expedient of the French gives them a manifest advantage. The French can stand more fatigue, keep their weapons longer, and rally with more ease when they are broken.

A very strong mortar battery is erecting within three hundred yards of the north-east part of Flushing. General Picton commands in this quarter. It is astonishing to us that the enemy have made no attempt to interrupt this work, as its conclusion must produce great effect. But there is a general opinion in the army, that the garrison are instructed to run no risks, but to keep the place as long as it is possible. The French marshals want only time to assemble their armies at Antwerp; and, what will not be very pleasing news to you, I am afraid they will have this time. The delay, however, does not rest with us. The whole force is required both at Lillo and at Flushing; of course we must take each in their turn.

In giving you these details of the siege, it would be unfair to omit the eminent services which we are daily receiving from the marine brigade under Lord A. Beauclerk; this brigade is composed of a detachment from all the men of war, who eagerly volunteer for the service. It amounts to nearly 500 men, and every man is a host. They have been particularly useful in bringing the heavy artillery from the vessels—a work of so much difficulty and time, that our present slow progress in the reduction of Flushing, is to be imputed to it. This artillery can only be landed at Campveer and must thence be dragged to Flushing, a distance of eight miles. The extent of our lines is nearly the whole breadth of the island; and by tomorrow night we expect to have one hundred pieces of artillery ready to play on the town.

From the delay which these circumstances have occasioned, the garrison of Flushing has received considerable reinforcements. The day before yesterday the gun-boats took a station which will prevent this in future; they were previously delayed by an unfavourable wind. My next letter will doubtless contain an account of the surrender of Flushing; for it is the confident opinion of all our best engineers, that it is impossible for the town to support the double bombardment by sea and land

Congreve is very busy with his rockets. I need not inform you that we are not very much prejudiced in favour of this new invention. I really think that they are scarcely fair weapons; and the principle, that of the introduction of more destructive instruments into the practise of war, should not be encouraged. They must necessarily become common; both parties are men on a level, and humanity only will be the sufferer. War already destructive, becomes more cruel. Such is our military opinion of Colonel Congreve's rockets.

Lord William Stuart has but this last hour taken his station with the frigates; he passed the two batteries of Cadsand and Flushing in grand style, and is now laying off the sea-front of Flushing. When they open on the town tomorrow, their effect must be dreadful.

The dikes have been cut, and the water begins to flow very fast. If Flushing do not fall within less than ten days, we must re-embark, or we shall be all drowned.

Such is the present state of our military operations; and having dispatched them, I shall continue my account of the island; you will find my information very correct; and, what must give it some value, I do not believe that you can procure it elsewhere. Our books of geography are lamentably deficient in details. Each follows the other, and; no one deems it necessary to do more than to change the form of what has been said by his predecessor. A few particulars on the ancient history of the towns of Middleburg and Flushing is all that I owe to the gazetteers and geographers.

The islands which compose the Province of Zealand are usually divided into those on the east bank of the Scheldt, and those on the west; and under the one or the other of these divisions, they may indeed, with some latitude of interpretation, be comprehended. In the distribution of a complicated and apparently unconnected subject, order is of so much importance, that it is excusable to strain a point to obtain it.

The islands of Zealand, on the West Scheldt, are four—Walcheren, North Beveland, South Beveland, and Wolversdyck.

Of these islands, Walcheren, if not the largest, is the most important. The island of Walcheren is about ten miles in length, and eight in breadth; it is the centre of all the islands at the mouth of the Scheldt, and exceeds them all in population, though South Beveland be of greater, extent. It is separated from the eastern branch of the Scheldt by the channel called the Veer-Gat, and some flats; and till the attempt of the English expedition, was deemed perfectly secure, on that side from all hostile attack. It is separated from South Beveland by a narrow channel, called the Slow, but which is navigable for ships of any burthen, though it has been erroneously stated otherwise in the *Gazettes* which the English Government issued on the occasion of the passage through it by the squadron of Sir Home Popham.

It is true, indeed, that the navigation is difficult in the extreme, and that this difficulty, unless remedied by the guidance of skilful pilots, almost, amounted to a complete defensive bulwark. It was perhaps fortunate for the British fleet that, in the confidence of their perfect security from any attempt on that side, the Dutch had neglected those precautions which might have rendered the Veer-Gat impassable. But it was not in this point only that the British expedition has been indebted to Fortune.

From the situation of Walcheren, it was notoriously the receptacle of smuggled goods; and perhaps it would not be too much to say, that almost every inhabitant either is, or has been supported by this indirect traffic. May it not, however, be a question, and a most important one, whether, in the present state of the Continent, to our manufacturers? If in certain branches of our commerce, bounties are willingly given to encourage exportation, may these not exist occasions in which these indirect drawbacks may be prudently connived at? If Walcheren be rendered a permanent member of the British Empire, it may become a matter of doubt whether the continental consumption of British goods would not be rather diminished than augmented.

Under the French Government the smugglers of Walcheren had no difficulty in transporting their British goods to Flanders, and thence into France. Now if Walcheren become a member of the British Empire, it will be necessary for France to have a standing and permanent army in Cadsand, and along both banks of the Scheldt. How are the Walcheren or English smugglers to elude this line of soldiery? So much for Walcheren becoming a depôt, whence English manufactures may be smuggled into the Continent. As far as this point is of importance, it would have been better to have left everything as it was. The smuggling trade could not have been in better hands than it was.

On the west side of the island of Walcheren is defended by downs, or sand-hills. On the other sides it is guarded from the sea by immense dikes which are so broad on the top, that two carriages may pass abreast. The expense of these dikes has been immense; and it might even be made a question, whether the price of thus fencing off their land be not double or treble what that land is worth. It is certain that, in some of the smaller islands, the human labour expended upon the dikes, if rated according to the price of labour in any other state of Europe, would more than purchase the fee simple of the land procured.

But the ancient Dutch had no alternative; they were pushed by their enemies to the shore of the ocean, and they then exerted themselves to scoop out a new empire. If we attempt to recall before our imaginations the scene which these islands must have presented previously to the erection of the dikes, the whole surface of them covered with a shallow sea, with only partial points of land here and there—if we endeavour to conceive these circumstances, we shall better be enabled to value the industry of the Dutch: no people in the world would have been capable of such an effort but these Hollanders.

The very repair of these dikes still continues a heavy tax on the inhabitants. Their height is proportioned to their thickness; notwithstanding which, the high tides sometimes pass over them, and when a storm concurs with the suitable age of the moon, the ravage has been dreadful. The sea, as seen from the dikes in one of these storms, is tremendous beyond description: the most extravagant picture of the poets does not exceed it. The waves seem curling over, and hastening onwards to bury the island and its inhabitants. The foreign visitor of the island cannot but feel a lively emotion of astonishment and alarm, when he sees them so near danger, and yet escaping from it. It is certain that nothing but their frequent escapes, and their habit of danger, could render them tranquil in such an abode.

Every square mile of Walcheren is intersected by canals or trenches, of which, from the habit of using them, the Dutch are so fond, that they convert them to nearly every purpose. A Dutchman will almost dig a canal for the conveyance of the dung from his stable to his garden. His house is, surrounded with moats. His garden is, fenced with one, and his orchard is defended by another. In the towns, the canal passes by his door, and brings the goods from every part of the island. This multitude of canals is productive of one great convenience, which almost overweighs the mischief of their stagnant waters. They serve as so many drains to the island, which is, thus dry and healthy in despite of its low situation. Without these drains, Walcheren would be an uninhabitable marsh.

The island of Walcheren produces everything which even an Englishman might deem necessary to the enjoyment of life, and everything is abundant, everything is very cheap. The prices indeed seem extraordinary when compared with those of England. Every article is at least one half or two-thirds less than what it would cost in England. There is the utmost abundance of fish; and the inhabitants avail themselves of this plenty, and of the ease with which it is obtained, to render it the principal component of their ordinary diet. Every meal in a Dutch house has one or more dishes of fish: fried, boiled, toasted, or merely dried; it always occupies its place at table.

On some of the banks and shallows, great quantities of oysters are periodically taken. This abundance of fish has necessarily a considerable influence on the flesh markets. The consumption of meat being diminished; the price of it falls in proportion. If an Englishman were only in pursuit of economy, he could not make a better choice for his residence than Walcheren. Fish, fowl, meat of all kinds, and flour are cheap to an extraordinary degree. Fuel, in fact, is the only article that is dear, and even for this there are many substitutes. If Walcheren, moreover, becomes a member of the British Empire, she may as before observed, be abundantly supplied from the British collieries.

Of all the islands of Zealand, Walcheren is the best wooded. The Dutch of Middleburg and Flushing, being in very opulent circumstances, have country-houses in that island; these they carefully ornament, and pursue this work with the characteristic perseverance of the Dutch character. The consequence is, that they obtain a victory over Nature; and accordingly groves, woods, and avenues are to be seen where Nature herself would not spontaneously grow a bush. Every part of the Island of Walcheren is shaded with these woods and groves. The island in this respect bears a near resemblance to the Isle of Thanet in England. Every square league has its village and every village its grove of trees surrounding, its church, and embosoming its houses. Nothing can be more delightful than the landscapes and scenery which are thus created. The favourite scenes of the Flemish painters may be recognised in every casual walk.

In the island of Walcheren almost in the lands belong to the possessors. There is nothing so painful to a Dutchman as living on the land or in the house of another. The first care of a Dutchman is to provide himself with a house of his own, a garden, a cow, and a wife. He is never easy till he has purchased the house or land on which he lives, and having once made the purchase, he holds it tight; death alone brings about alienation, and his heirs receive the price. The lands in Walcheren therefore almost invariably belong to the possessors; they are usually very small properties, and bear a large price. Leases, the laws of landlord and tenant, and indeed almost the very name of lawyers or advocates, are unknown amongst them; they have a passionate aversion to litigation, and subject everything to a kind of commercial arbitration. It is considered as infamous to oppose the offer of such reference: manners have here greater weight than positive laws.

The inhabitants of the island of Walcheren have a peculiar character superinduced over their national character as Dutchmen. They are very brave and very manly; but that is all that can be said on the favourable side. They are cunning, and fraudulent and follow their own interest in despite of every moral restraint. Being all smugglers, they have a kind of habitual contempt of law, and seem to consider everything as just which they can commit with impunity. If the English revenue law shall be extended to Walcheren, and be executed with as much severity as in England, half the inhabitants in the island would shortly be under a Crown prosecution. They have absolutely no conception of any criminality in the most atrocious smuggling. They appear to deem all law as so much unjust restraint, and unauthorized imposition, and that therefore it is ever laudable to elude it. In this kind of morality, indeed the Englishmen on the Sussex and Kentish coast keep them in countenance. There is, in fact, no room for a choice between them.

Previous to the war, the island of Walcheren carried on a very brisk trade, and particularly in what is termed the dry provision trade. A great quantity of Dutch cheeses, and many ship-loads of bacon, hams, and potted butter, were weekly sent to the opposite coast of England, and particularly to Yarmouth in Norfolk, where there was an established fair, once or twice in. the year, for these Dutch importations. The merchants of Middleburg and Flushing moreover had a very extensive business in the fishery, and by their superior management, and more economical method of drying and preserving, were enabled considerably to undersell us in Spain and Portugal. The quantity of dried fish which these merchants annually send into America is incredible; and, in despite of the English navigation laws, even our colonies were, in good part supplied from the Dutch fishery.

The English Parliament had become jealous of this commercial participation and intrusion; and even if the war had not broken out when it did, the good understanding of the two nations would not long have continued. England and Holland have long had a jealous contention in commerce, in the same manner as England and France have contended for political rank and predominance. This spirit still continues, and the Dutch will continue to hate us as long as we retain their colonies. The loss of the Cape of Good Hope hangs heavy upon them.

Since the commencement of the war, Walcheren has carried on two branches of trade: the one a permissive trade under an assumed flag, in provisions; the other, a more considerable and lucrative trade in smuggling from England into France, and from France into England. There are many English and Scotch families settled in the island, who cannot have any other possible business there, but to conduct and to facilitate this trade. The English Government will doubtless consider before they extend the English revenue laws to their new conquest. This smuggling may be less injurious than it has been considered. The present are times in which many old maxims have been successfully disputed.

There are three principal towns in the Island of Walcheren—Campveer, Middleburg, and Flushing.

Campveer, which is laid down in all the English maps as Ter Veer, is a very ancient and considerable town, and under the former Republican Government of the States, had a vote in the General Assembly. It is situated very pleasantly in an open but well-wooded country; it is at a small distance from the mouth of the Scheldt, and the possession of it, and of the fort in its vicinity, Haak or Der Haak, would enable any power to enter the East Scheldt at pleasure. The Veer-Gat indeed abounds in sand-flats and shallows; but there is so little obstruction to the navigation, that the largest ships may pass, and almost daily have passed into the Slow, and thence to Flushing.

The depth of the Veer-Gat, close to the Walcheren coast, is very considerable, and to those who know the channel, there is neither difficulty nor danger in the attempt. The danger, however, is very great, unless with a skilful pilot, and with due precaution. Ships even of tolerable burthen must proceed, very slowly and very cautiously in their passage to Campveer. Accidents have frequently happened, though the Government of the island have neglected no means to secure their shipping. On the whole line of the coast of the Island of Walcheren, there are light-houses at short and nearly equal distances. The main danger, however, is when the rise of the sea is so great, that the ship is actually above the surface of the land, so that nothing can be seen, even in the immediate vicinity of the land, but sea and sky.

This town derives its name of Campveer from having anciently been the ferry to the town of Campen on the island of North Beveland; but this latter town is now so completely washed away, that scarcely one stone remains upon another. Many of these towns have indeed disappeared, both on the coast of Walcheren, and on that of the opposite islands. Perhaps nowhere has the sea more fully exhibited its tremendous power, and nowhere has it been more successfully checked. The whole Province of Zealand, in an era not far distant, must have been at the bottom of the sea. What an extraordinary proof does it now present, of what may be effected by human industry! Are not the dikes of Holland more honourable to the Dutch, than the Pyramids to the Egyptians?

It is unnecessary to add, that Campveer is inferior in magnitude, in importance, in strength, in everything but pleasantness of situation, to either Flushing or Middleburg. Campveer in fact, is only the third town of the province, and therefore must not be brought into competition with the other two; but Campveer has one praise which cannot be extended to Flushing—it is proverbially the healthiest place of the island, brisk, opulent, and clean. The Dutch, much to their credit, value their towns as much according to the cleanliness of their inhabitants, as from any other quality whatever; and the housewives of Campveer have so well maintained the reputation of the town, that it is the favourite resort of the island. A week's residence at Campveer is the country recess of the rich Flushinger.

The works of Campveer are respectable, but are not very

strong; they are sufficient to protect it against any surprise, but are not equal to a permanent defence. The fortifications, however, considering what they are, reflect much credit on the engineer. They are sufficient to enable the garrison to withstand a force quadruple to themselves, and to give a warm reception to an assaulting enemy. No garrison, however, could be mad enough to hold Campveer beyond a day or two against a force greatly superior to them; and particularly when it is always in their power to retreat to Flushing, and to make their stand there.

In time of peace, Campveer carries on a very brisk trade, and particularly, with Scotland. In time of war, this trade is exchanged for smuggling traffic, in which the inhabitants of Campveer are a kind of partners with the Englishmen on the opposite side of the water. The boats of Campveer go out to meet the English boys, and each are laden and unladen at sea. An immense quantity of French goods and spirits was thus conveyed into England, and particularly lace of all qualities, silk, &c. There is some reason to believe that this trade was encouraged by the French Government. It certainly answered the purposes of France, and procured an issue and sale for their commodities.

Campveer is particularly distinguished amongst the Dutch towns as being the residence of many opulent Scotch families, some of them very respectable, some of them merely opulent. The motives which have led these Scotchmen to become Dutch *denizens*, and fixed inhabitants of Walcheren, are not difficult to be assigned, They have doubtless originally settled there as the agents or partners of smuggling firms in England and Scotland. Many of them were active in carrying on this traffic down to the moment of the arrival of the English Expedition and have made immense fortunes, have retired from business, and many having died, have left noble fortunes to their families.

These latter having no further occasion to continue in the same course, become respectable; but with the characteristic nature of Scotchmen, preserve all their Scotch habits in the midst of a foreign people. Every Englishman is received by them as a countryman, and every Scotchman as a brother. The extent, to which the smuggling trade was carried on, is beyond all possible belief. The Scotch residents constituted a kind of factory, through which, as a medium, the business was managed on both sides. The conquest of the island must necessarily terminate this traffic; but it will still be a question whether the English manufactures will gain or lose by this interruption of their smuggling customers.

Four miles from Campveer along the coast is the town of Armyden. The road to it is the coast road to Flushing. Armyden was, anciently a very large and thriving town; but the mouth of its harbour having been filled up, it at present resembles rather a village than a town. It still, however, takes the lead of the smaller towns in the Island of Walcheren, and, like all Dutch towns, is fresh, cleanly, and brisk-looking. Nothing can, in fact, be more pleasing to the eye than the Dutch country towns. They are usually broad, the paths paved with bricks and porches before the houses. The windows are shaded by trees, of which the Dutch are particularly careful.

After a spring or a summer shower, when the trees are divested of their dust, and the sun shines on them, nothing can be more gay and animated than the scene which they present. In the summer evening, the fathers and uncles usually smoke their pipes in these porches, whilst the younger people are parading up and down the town. The Dutch manners and diversions are certainly more sober than those of the French; but ease and happiness are the same everywhere, and the Dutchman, with his pipe, his bowl, his dried fish, and his Hague Courant, is as happy, if not as noisy, as the Frenchman.

In a military point of view, Armyden is totally defenceless. It is merely an open town or village; it was anciently much stronger than at present. The present town indeed is not the same as the old one of the same name. Nothing of the latter remains but its site, and a few old walls, by the side of a small river or canal, called the Arne, whence indeed the name of the town is derived.

From Armyden to Middleburg is two miles and a half. Middleburg is not only the capital of Walcheren, but of the whole Province of Zealand. It was a very old town; but having been constantly repaired, has all the freshness and external cleanliness of a modern city. It is termed Middleburg, from its situation in the centre of the island.

By means of its canal, which is a mile and a half in length, it communicates with the Veer-Gat, the Slow, and of course with the Western Scheldt. This canal was cut in the year 1533, and is deep and capacious enough to admit the largest ships up to the town. Connected with this canal, are the town basin, and the moats which protected the city during the Spanish war.

The ancient history of the town would require a volume to itself. It was originally only a village, which the Lords of Borssell augmented, and in the year 1132 surrounded with walls. Several circumstances have concurred to render it what it is at present. The Town House is a very magnificent building, and is ornamented with a great number of statues of the ancient Counts and Countesses of Holland. According to what is related in the history of the town, this Town House was originally an abbey, founded in the middle of the 13th century by William, King of the Romans, and Count of Holland and Zealand. The body of this Prince, illustrious for his piety and his rank, is interred in one of the churches of the town, and a most magnificent monument has been therein raised to his memory, by Florent the Fifth.

In this church was held a chapter of the order of the Golden Fleece, in 1505, by Philip the Fair, Duke of Burgundy, afterwards King of Spain, when he created ten knights. It was destroyed by lightning in the year 1712. The revenues of the Abbey were granted to the Bishop when Pope Paul IV established an Episcopal see at Middleburg in 1562, and the Collegiate Church of St. Peter was made a cathedral. The diocese was under the Archbishopric of Utrecht, and its jurisdiction extended over ten cities, and about a hundred villages, and was divided into four deaneries, in which were included nine chapters of Canons; one Abbey, and thirty-three, monasteries.

The Bishopric continued but a very short time; for in the year 1574 the city was taken by the Hollanders, after a siege of twenty-two months; during which it was bravely defended by Christopher de Montdragon, the Spanish general, who, after enduring extreme hardships, surrendered, on the terms that the sacred vessels, church ornaments, ecclesiastics, and the garrison, should be safely conducted to Flanders, and that the Baron of Ste. Aldegonde, the intimate friend of the Prince of Orange, who had been taken prisoner by the Spaniards, should be set at liberty; which were faithfully executed by both parties. Since that time the reformed religion has taken place, and the Bishopric been dissolved, Spain made every possible effort to oblige the Hollanders to raise the siege, and expended vast sums in fitting out diverse fleets and armaments to, succour the inhabitants; but they were all defeated by the brave Zealanders.

The fortifications of Middleburg are very strong and regular, having been much augmented by the Dutch since they became masters of it. They have eight gates, and twelve bastions to defend the walls and ramparts, with large and deep ditches filled with water; besides which, its situation is such as to enable the inhabitants to lay the country about it under water when they please.

Middleburg has many other public buildings; but since the French came into the possession of the town, they converted them to other purposes. The public buildings in Holland are notoriously superior to anything of the kind in England. The Republic, in the days of its splendour, spared no expense in anything of a public nature. Hence the stranger will find much to interest him in a walk over this town. If Middleburg should become a garrison for the English soldiery, these buildings might be converted into noble barracks. The Admiralty College, the Chamber of Accounts, and the Mint are worthy of the character of the Dutch. They are noble buildings and are preserved with the care which they merit.

Middleburg divides the trade of the island with Flushing. The merchants of Middleburg are perhaps of a more respectable character than those of Flushing; the greater part of those at Flushing having made their fortunes by smuggling, and therefore are people of low habits. Those of Middleburg come nearer to the idea which the English have of Dutch merchants. There are many delightful promenades in the immediate vicinity of Middleburg; but the one of the most resort is the road from Middleburg to Flushing, which on both sides is beautifully planted with trees. From Flushing to Middleburg is about five miles, and the whole interval resembles an ornamental avenue. The neatness of the fields and gardens, and country-houses along each side of this road, is peculiarly striking to an Englishman. In the spring and summer nothing can be more gay than the meadows along this road. The townspeople and their children are sporting over them, young people at their accustomed pastimes, and their elder parents and relations walking with the characteristic sedateness of the Dutch.

This walk, which is the; usual summer promenade, is generally terminated at Flushing—a town which resembles Middleburg in its magnitude and antiquity, but differs much from it in its characteristic style. Flushing may be taken as a model of a Dutch town. The English traveller, immediately on entering it, is struck with something which he had never seen before. The houses are built of very small bricks, they are unusually lofty, are filled with large windows, and project forwards, so as to be some feet from the perpendicular. They remind an Englishman of old farmhouses, or rather of those old mansions which in the northern parts of England are termed halls. The bricks, however, being constantly pointed, give them a neatness which peculiarly contrasts with their antiquity.

The person, who walks in the street, is secure enough from a shower; he is likewise sheltered from the sun; but before he has been in some degree accustomed to the place, it is impossible to divest himself at an apprehension, that houses so declining from a perpendicular elevation, may fall upon his head.

Every town in Holland has trees intermixed with the houses. The Dutch are so fond of this ornament, that they very willingly forego air and light, that they may have shade and shelter. This ornament, added to their cleanliness, gives an air of peculiar freshness to a Dutch town. The trees, moreover, act as a kind of fan in the hot weather; and there is a current opinion, and an established saying, that they exhale a perfume which is salutary to the health and to the spirits.

Many of the houses in Flushing are in nothing inferior to those of Rotterdam; like those of Rotterdam, they belong to merchants who have made their fortunes on the spot, and who live where they have made their money. Many of these kind of people, having realized the fortunes of Princes, content themselves with a tasteless but expensive enlargement of their paternal house, adding room to room, but in all transmutations carefully retaining something of the original structure. Some of these houses have thus a curious appearance, and more particularly so, as every Dutchman adds some caprice of his own; perhaps on the top of his house he will erect a room in the shape of a punch-bowl, or more frequently of a ship; in a word, anything which may recall to his mind the means or instruments of his fortune.

The fortifications of Flushing are very strong, and if the town be well provisioned, that is to say, be not attacked by surprise, it is calculated to hold out for a great length of time. Flushing, however, cannot be long retained against an army in Flanders, the channel being so narrow, as to be easily passed. The harbour of Flushing is nearly 100 yards in length; it was made at the general expense of the States, and is capable of holding an immense navy, and of protecting them when they are there. Eighty ships of war have occasionally laid there in the period of the naval glory of the Dutch. To the right of the New Haven, leading to the Provincial Basin, is a large dock; and to the westward of this dock, lies the entrance into the Old Harbour, which is divided into two departments, and serves for merchant ships.

There are three churches, all of them of the Calvinistic persuasion. There is one characteristic distinction in all Dutch churches—the walls are covered with the escutcheons of the dead. Even the French Revolution has not removed this custom: the Dutch have still so much family pride, that they rejoice to be considered as the descendants from families or individuals who have signalized themselves in the Spanish wars.

As to the ancient history of the town, it is sufficient to observe that the origin of the prosperity of Flushing was immediately after the Spanish wars. Previous to the year 1572 Flushing was little better than a village or small hamlet, being a mere ferry over to Flanders; but its inhabitants behaved so well, and were so serviceable in annoying the Spaniards, that an unanimous vote of the States admitted it into the number of the voting towns. This celebrity, added to its advantageous situation, soon rendered it a favourite residence; it was shortly afterwards fortified, embellished with public edifices, and endowed with a charter of many valuable privileges. In the year 1589 it was mortgaged to Queen Elizabeth, of England, in conjunction with Briel and Rammekins; and in consequence thereof received an English garrison. The loan being repaid, it was restored to the States by James I.

It must not be omitted in an account of the present state of this town, that its inhabitants are not of the most respectable kinds; that too many of them are smugglers; and many of them, without any interest in the war, are owners of privateers, with which they act the part of freebooters on the ocean. The habits of smuggling are not favourable to the morals of a people. It is a frequent and just remark that every business which requires privacy is injurious to morals. The inhabitants of Flushing are accordingly considered as very low on the moral scale; but this certainly must not be applied to all.

Yours &c.

Letter 7

Middleburg, Aug; 12, 1809.
My Dear Sir,

You must consider this as the continuation of my former letter. We are not allowed to sleep, and therefore we may as well employ our nights in one way as well as another. Of all people in the world, the French support an attack best. We have the advantage of them in numbers, in artillery, in the courage of our men, and in the skill of our engineers (I speak only of our present expedition); and yet with all these circumstances before their eyes, and knowing, moreover, that they must surrender, they still continue to hold a good face on it, and I am persuaded will not surrender till the very last extremity.

This extremity, however, will be the commencement of our sea bombardment. I will tell you a secret—it must not pass further—were it not for our ships, Flushing could not be taken. Our land-forces have little to do but to shut up the enemy within their walls, and be ready to take possession of the city when it shall have struck to the ships. Five thousand men would have executed this service as well as fifty thousand. This is my opinion.

Our condition becomes very uncomfortable. We are already knee-deep in water; and unless the city surrenders before the end of the next week, we must re-embark. The water begins to flow so fast, that there is scarcely an inch of dry ground. All the fresh water of the island, moreover, is spoiled; everything else is abundant. Provisions are infinitely cheaper, than they are in England; the land is very fertile, and the cheapness is proportionate to the plenty. In dry weather, as I have said before, the island of Walcheren must be a delightful place—the scenery so animated, and the cultivation so careful and minute. The fields are weeded like the gardens, and the gardens are as regularly cleaned as the rooms of the houses. The first moral duty of a Dutch housewife seems to be cleanliness. The brush and mop are in continual revolution.

Our soldiers annoy the peasantry extremely. We have hourly complaints that they enter their houses without taking off their shoes; upon this subject, however—the conduct of our soldiers in foreign quarters—it is but justice to say, that the French soldiers are under stricter discipline, and more obedient to it. Our brave fellows are too apt to suffer their contempt of every country but their own, to urge them to acts of insult and outrage in their foreign quarters. Our principal trouble, however, is to restrain them with respect to the women. Plunder is rare; but this personal kind of outrage so common, and so general, as almost to defy any efforts to prevent it.

Lord Chatham passes almost the whole of his time in Middleburg, which has become a very agreeable place. The inhabitants, indeed, are not very social; but they sell their commodities for money, and this is all we have to expect of them.

From the flowing of the waters, above and below, for it rains incessantly, we begin to suffer very much in our health. You can almost see this exhalations as they rise, and you may most assuredly smell them. Nothing can be so insufferable as the stench of the hollows. I have no doubt but that if Flushing be taken, and an English garrison be stationed there, the mortality will be very great. There is a kind of pestilence which is said to prevail here in the autumn. We already begin to feel its effects even in the open country. Not a regiment is to be found but what has suffered considerably; nearly the whole of the 23rd Regiment is in the hospitals. The sentinels are sometimes relieved twice instead of once, by reason of the sudden indisposition of the men. I confess that this increasing disease has alarmed me exceedingly. Men are frequently carried from the parade.

The attack is sudden and violent; the prevalent diseases are the dysentery and the intermittent. They of course originate in the infected-air and in the unwholesome water. The climate for this last week has been variable in the extreme. In the morning it rains heavily—at noon there is burning sun, which covers one with perspiration. The nights, again, become extremely cold; but the cold damps and the hot damps are the most perilous;—the former spread rheumatisms and the latter are absolutely pestilential.

You will perceive that this varies from my former statement of the general healthiness of this island. I have no other excuse, than that in my former letters I wrote from report; it was impossible, indeed, that I should speak from experience. Fatal experience has now come; our men are dying hourly, and almost by the minute; and an order has just been issued, doubtless from this frequency, that all burials shall be by night, and without candles or torches. The lines really begin to resemble the Grecian camp. The 26th Regiment has likewise suffered most dreadfully; upwards of 250 men are declared unfit for duty, and perhaps a great proportion of this number will never be fit for duty again. How is it possible, indeed, to avoid disease, when, added to the variable nature of the climate, not an inch of dry ground is to be found in the island? We are for hours together up to our knees in water.

You will confess that all this is but a very bad prospect of our future success; and I can assure you that some of our officers begin to wear very long faces. One complaint is general, that Sir John Hope has waited in Beveland the reduction of Flushing. There is a general opinion that he should have been sent to Lillo and Antwerp. It is urged, indeed, on the other hand, that the naval flotilla of the enemy in the Scheldt is too strong for us, and I am afraid that there is some, truth in this. Be it as it may, things begin to have a gloomy air. Flushing, however, will be ours in two or three days.

I now resume my account of Walcheren and the other islands. Do me the favour to keep my letters, as they may assist my recollection upon my return to England.

I have already given you a cursory account of Middleburg, Flushing, Campveer, and Armyden.

The town next in importance to Walcheren is West Capelle, about six miles from Middleburg, and eight from Flushing. The Dutch seem very fond of ornamenting their roads, and rendering them agreeable promenades. From every town and every village you will see roads in all directions and as carefully ornamented and cleaned as if they were so many garden walls; every pebble larger than what constitutes the groundwork of the road, is carefully removed; and when the surface of the road is over a plain, there would be no obstacle to a ball running from one end of it to the other. In summer, moreover, these roads are all watered; and in winter, I believe, they have some contrivance for keeping them dry. Small villas decorate each side, and every villa has its garden.

Nothing, however, can be more tasteless than the ornaments in a Dutch garden; leaden Mercuries and painted jolly Venuses stand under every tree. The lawns, however, are carefully mown; and where there are gravel-walks, they always look as if fresh made. The flowers, moreover, are in a plenty and luxuriance which astonish a foreigner. The Dutch carry this fondness for flowers to the wildest extravagance. It is no uncommon thing for them to sell or buy a pink or a rose at a sum equal to an hundred pounds English. The Loves of the Plants are here verified.

Much of the beauty of the island of Walcheren arise from these flower-gardens, which I am thus minute in describing, because they constitute a scenery which is perfectly strange to an English eye. Every respectable inhabitant in Middleburg and Flushing has his garden along some of the country roads; and on every Sunday, or other, holiday, spends nearly the whole of his day there.

In the summer evenings, moreover, these gardens are the end and objects of their walks. A Dutchman envies no one whilst he is sitting in state in one of the arbours, or looking from the window of his summer-house; and the younger part of his family, whilst playing around him, seems as happy as himself. You have, doubtless, remarked in all the paintings of the ancient Dutch School a peculiar luxuriance of natural scenery, and that general air and character of landscape, which the painters term rest. Every scene in Walcheren reminds you of this scenery. You would scarcely imagine how so small a spot could be rendered so delightfully picturesque. To say all in a word, it reminds one of an highly cultivated garden—there is no waste, no neglect.

The Dutch, moreover, are never satisfied with one road to any given point. They must have a water road as well as a land road. Every town has its canal as well as its road. This multitude of canals; however, has an advantage which I have before mentioned—that of draining the country. In the country, moreover, this beneficial effect is not counteracted by the filth which in the towns is invariably thrown into the canals. In Flushing and Middleburg the canals smell like so many sewers. Every kind of garbage is thrown into them; and they resemble horse-ponds rather than streams of water. This is not the case in the country canals.

Whilst I am mentioning the scenery along the roads, I must not omit another trait which characterizes a Dutch landscape: Gipsies, beggars, and vagrants are unknown. The poor-laws in Walcheren, and I believe throughout Holland, are upon the same footing as in England; every parish supports its own poor, and the annual expense of such support is levied by a rate on the house-holders. I should imagine, however, from what I see, that this annual amount is but small. The lower orders of the Dutch have a peculiar pride. In Walcheren, moreover, there are so many means of procuring a livelihood, that none but the most worthless could be absolutely destitute. I am happy, however, to have it in my power to add, that the Dutch are naturally a very charitable people.

Another object of novelty to the traveller in Walcheren, and which you see in every road, and almost in every field, is the stork, and the bird called the heron. These birds are doubtless invited here by the great abundance of water. The Dutch seem to hold them in almost as much veneration as the Turks and Egyptians; and the birds themselves seem to have a kind of Dutch air and heaviness. The climate certainly extends beyond mere human nature.

You may perhaps imagine that we must have too much employment to have any time to walk into the country; but this is not true—the operations have been so long delayed, that the greater part of us have little to do but to look on as spectators. As to our commander in chief, he spends the greater part of his time in Middleburg, and very freely and good-naturedly permits the officers to follow their own inclinations. So much I must say of him that everyone seems to feel a lively regard for him; his manners are so gentlemanlike, and his temper so easy and affable, that he has at least won all our hearts. But there are certainly some murmurs that he is not sufficiently decisive, that he wants confidence in his own powers, that he is too fond of councils of war, and that he is deliberating, where the nature of the service required that he should be acting.

Be this as it may, he is the perfect gentleman; and when he thinks proper to exert himself, an excellent officer. Everyone acknowledge his abilities, whilst they lament that he does not sufficiently put them forth. I have heard that the late Lord Chatham, the great Chatham as he is deservedly called, entertained a very high opinion of our commander's abilities. The late Lord Clarendon being one day at his house, and Mr. Pitt and Lord Chatham, at that time boys, happening to pass—"There, my Lord," said Lord Chatham, "are my best services to my country; there are two boys who will hereafter be most useful men. The one, Mr. Pitt, is the readiest; he has a due confidence in himself. The other will be the most solid thinker."

To return, however, to the thread of my subject—the topography of Walcheren. A few miles from East Capelle is West Capelle, a town of more importance, if importance be measured rather by ancient repute, than by existing fortune. West Capelle has been raised to fame by the repeated mention of it in the ancient history of Holland. It is situated on the western side of the island, which has been fenced off by a very strong dike; all the sand-hills and downs having been, gradually washed away by the encroachment of the sea.

This town has nothing to recommend it to notice, except that it be a most obstinate and bloody engagement which was fought here in the time of William II. Count of Holland, between the army of that Prince, and that of Margaret Countess of Flanders, surnamed the Black. The Flemish army was defeated with great slaughter.

Three miles from Armyden, along the same coasts is the town of Domburg; it is a brisk, lively town, situated amongst the sand-hills, and therefore very low, and perfectly defenceless.

There are but two forts on the Island of Walcheren—Rammekins, and Der Haak or Haak. Neither of them is of greater strength than is sufficient to repel a single ship of the line. The great strength of the island are the fortifications of Flushing.

That I may give you a complete topographical view of the island, I shall briefly mention that the following country towns and villages are all contained in the island—East Capelle, Kleverskerke, Breedame, St. Laurens, containing the ruins of the celebrated old Castle of Popkensburg; Gaveren, containing another old castle; Serooskerke, Polder, Grypskerke, Sagtkerke, Mileskerke, Riggerkerke, Konderkerke, Zoatelande, West Zouburg, and Rithem. At a small distance from Campveer are to be seen the remains of the old Castle of Zandberg, an ancient possession of the House of Orange. In addition to the above is the islet of Jostland, which is divided from Walcheren by a narrow sluice or channel. This islet contains only one village, that of Nieuwland.

From the Island of Walcheren, the traveller in the Dutch Province of Zealand will pass over to South Beveland, which is only separated from Walcheren by the narrow channel of the Slow. The Island of South Beveland is the largest and pleasantest of all the islands which constitute this province. It was formerly indeed much larger than at present, extending itself as far as the East Scheldt; but in the year 1532, the eastern part was laid, under water by the breaking in of the waves, attended by a fierce storm; since which, the dikes have never been restored, and accordingly in all the maps, this part is denominated by the name of the Drowned Land.

In this over-flowed country stood, an ancient town of the name of Romerswaal, where King Philip II of Spain was installed Count of Zealand. This town was shortly afterwards burned down by the Spaniards, and has been subsequently washed away. The capital city of South Beveland is Goes, which is situated in the most northern part of the island, not far from the East Scheldt, with which it communicates by means of an harbour or canal, denominated the New Haven. This name has been given to it by way of distinction from the Old, the mouth of which having been choked up with sand. It serves at present only to keep the New Harbour always fit for service; and accordingly a sluice has been built on the intermediate dam, which, in time of flood, is opened for the water to run but of the New Haven into the Old; after which the sluice is again shut, and is not opened till the ebb has left the New Harbour dry; then the water which has been withheld, rushes with such impetuosity out of the Old Harbour, through the New, towards the Scheldt, that it carries off all the sand and mud, and preserves a proper depth of water in the New Harbour.

Goes has some fortifications, but not such as can enable it to hold out against an enemy of any force. It is a brisk trading town, particularly for salt. It is a town of little consequence in a military point of view.

The next town of importance in Beveland is Monster, commonly called Borselen. This town was formerly much larger than at present; but the old town was destroyed, in good part, by the inundation which drowned so considerable a portion of the country. The country indeed has been since diked; but Monster is still occasionally flooded, and therefore an unpleasant and unsafe habitation. This part of the country bears a strong resemblance to the town of Romney in Kent, but is not so unwholesome, and is more plentiful in provisions.

Capelle is the third town of Beveland; it is situated in a beautiful neighbourhood, and there are some delightful walks amongst some ancient ruins in its immediate vicinity. The Isles of Zealand are peculiarly characterized by their ancient castles, many of which are coeval with the heroic ages, and necessarily recall to the well-read traveller the days of feudal glory. On the battlements of these castles the Barons of ancient times would watch the rising of the tempestuous ocean around them, and, safe in their massy walls, mark the fury of the winds and waves. In other castles; acts of ferocity have been committed, which have rendered the walls hateful even to the present day.

The verdure of South Beveland cannot be exceeded, perhaps not equalled, in England. It produces an abundance of everything which can contribute to the sustenance or enjoyment of man; and the inhabitants have the reputation of being a milder race of people than those of Flushing. Perhaps having less opportunities of smuggling, their morals are more pure, as their actual temptations are less.

Schore, Vlake, Kluningen, Oudeland, and Barland are villages or hamlets, and have nothing to distinguish them. Bathz is a fort and hamlet, not very strong; it is situated on the entrance of Beveland towards Lillo.

The third island at the mouth of the Scheldt is Wolversdyck, which is situated between North and South Beveland, and is separated from the one by the channel called the South Deep, and from the other by that part of the Scheldt which is termed the Schenge. This islet is very small, and contains only one town, called Oosterland.

The fourth island in the opening of the Scheldt, is North Beveland, which is separated from Wolversdyck by the channel called the South Fleet, This island was once the most pleasant and fertile country in all Zealand; but in the years 1530 and 1532 it suffered such a terrible inundation, that an immense number of persons and cattle perished; and of the whole island nothing was to be seen but the spire, or pinnacle, of one steeple, which just appeared above the summit, of the waters. About a century afterwards, the ground being raised by the continual increase, of the mud, the island was again diked in, and cultivated. This island has but two towns—Kortjyn, a country town, formerly the patrimony of the *Stadtholder*; and Wissenkerke, a mere village.

West of North Beveland is the narrow channel of Bompot, between two sandbanks, called Onrush and Scotsman. This is the only passage for all vessels bound from Holland to Middleburg; but when the weather is in the least foul, it is very dangerous to those who are not thoroughly acquainted with it The channel north of North Beveland is also called the Bompot.

All the above islands, except Walcheren, are full of marshes, which are not without their advantages, as yielding good turf for fuel; and in many parts of Zealand, the marshes are reckoned the best defences of the country. These morasses, however, joined with the low situation of the country near the sea, occasion a damp air and frequent rains, which, as well as the thick fogs here are more particularly brought on by the westerly winds, which prevail for a considerable part of the year in these quarters. Should an English garrison, therefore, be stationed in any of these islands, there would certainly be reason for apprehension that they would suffer much from the manual distempers, of the island.

The Islands of Zealand, as I have before mentioned, are distributed into two divisions, those on the West Scheldt, and those on the East Walcheren, North and South Beveland, and Wolversdyck, belong to the west division.

The east division comprehends the four following islands: Schowen, Duyveland, Ter Tholen, and St. Philip's Land.

Of these the Island of Schowen is the most important. This island formerly extended much farther towards the southward; and the East Scheldt, by which it is separated from the North Beveland, was at that time so narrow, that the inhabitants of the two islands could converse together from the opposite sides; but the stream has insensibly encroached so much on the land, that in some parts it is a Dutch mile in breadth.

The land of this island, as well as that of Duyveland, of which we shall speak hereafter, lies very level, and in many places considerably beneath the bed of the sea; for which reason it is not only fenced against inundations by dikes and dams, at a most prodigious expense, but a still more enormous expense is incurred by drains, without which the greater part of the land would be still uninhabitable. Every inch of this island may be described as land scooped out by human industry from the bed of the ocean.

In the island of Schowen are only two towns of any consequence—Zirksee and Brouwershaven.

Zirksee is a very considerable town, and under the ancient Government of the island, had a vote in the States. It is very advantageously situated for maritime trade, as communicating with the East Scheldt by means of the New Haven. Accordingly it enjoys, or in time of peace it did enjoy, a very brisk trade, having sometimes so many as seventy or eighty ships of its own, which are usually freighted to all parts of the world.

The domestic trade of the place is in salt and mead, of which the island prepares and produces great quantities. Within the town, moreover, are several pits for keeping oysters, besides other grounds for their growth; and immense quantities of them are sent to other provinces and to foreign countries. In a word, the inhabitants neglect nothing by which they can make money. Zirksee is considered by the inhabitants as the most ancient town in all Zealand; and amidst many other calamities by which it has suffered, one-half of it in the year 1414 was burnt down.

Brouwershaven is a town of inferior dimensions; it is situated on the Grevelinjen water, and the greater part of its inhabitants are seamen or fishermen. Its chief business is the oyster trade, having some very considerable beds. This town has suffered much both by fire and water. It was likewise the scene of a most dreadful and remarkable battle, which, in the year 1420, was fought hereabouts between Philip Duke of Burgundy, and Humphrey Duke of Gloucester, at which time it was only a village.

The traveller in the island of Schowen would not fail to remark the many ruins of towns which were formerly distinguished and populous, but which are now under water, and with scarcely one stone upon another. The character of the Dutch, their rigid industry, and their unwearied perseverance are peculiarly conspicuous in this island. Here are immense dikes, which, often destroyed, have been as often restored, and with such increased strength after every successive ruin, as at last to be enabled to withstand the winds and waves.

I shall mention the names of the villages of this island, as some of them may possibly become the scene of future operations. The following are those only which deserve a mention:—Dryschor, Ellmeet, Haamsted, Jerooskerke, Wellande, Polder, and Zenipe. Haamsted is a beautiful village, fresh, cleanly, and thriving. In the neighbourhood of Renisse is an old castle, termed Moermond.

Burght and Naamste are two hamlets which may merit mention.

The island of Duyveland is the second island on the East Scheldt; the channel which separates it from Schowen is called the Dyke-water. The channel to the south-ward is called the Keten, and that to the eastward is termed Waadays, which is, a passage for all vessels bound from Holland to Zealand. The island itself owes its name to the great number of *doyven*; or pigeons, with which it formerly abounded. In the year 1530 it was overflowed by the sea with such rapidity, that besides cattle, some hundreds of persons perished by the waters. Not long after, however, it was again diked in. There are no places on it of sufficient consequence to be denominated towns; there are five villages, the names of which are as follow:—Nieuwerkerke, Oudiskerke, Capelle, Botland, Heer Janstand, and Bruinesse, The last village and its districts are sometimes termed East Duyveland. The island of Duyveland is four miles in length, and two in breadth.

The low and watery island of Ter Tholen is of about the same dimensions, and contains the following towns—Ter Tholen and St. Martensdyke.

Ter Tholen is a very principal town, and under the ancient Government had a vote in the States. It lies on the River Endracht, on the other side of which it has a groundwork, and towards the land-side it is fortified with a rampart and seven bastions. It has two large churches. In 1712 Tholen was surprised and plundered by the French.

St. Martensdyke was part of the patrimony of William the Third of England; it is now little better than a village or hamlet, though formerly of more consequence. It has no fortifications, and few inhabitants. The villages of this island are Stavenisse, Skerpenisse, St. Anneland, Westkerke, Portvliet, and Old Vasmar. Off the village of Stavenisse there was a naval engagement between the Spaniards and the Netherlanders, in which Hollard, the Zealand Admiral, took seventy-six flat-bottomed boats, and made upwards of four thousand prisoners.

The fourth island on the eastern bank of the Scheldt is St. Philip's Land, which contains only one village, which is of the same name with itself.

The before-mentioned islands, Walcheren, North Beveland, Duyveland, Tolen Land, Wolversdyck, South Beveland, and St. Philip's Land are all the islands which form the mouth of the Scheldt, and constitute the Province of Zealand. Where these islands terminate, *i. e.* at the southern extremity of South Beveland, the two arms of the Scheldt unite in the body of the river, and one noble and undivided; stream rolls down to Antwerp. From Sanvliet, where the body of the river recommences, to Antwerp, is thirteen miles; and during the whole of this line, on both sides of the river, is a chain of forts, each distant from the other about one mile.

The following are the names of these forts, with their general condition as to actual strength.

Fort Sanvliet.—this fort is very strong, and cannot be passed by shipping.

Fort Henry.—this fort has been demolished.

Fort Blacugarten.—this fort is likewise very strong, and in good condition.

Fort Lillo.—this is a most important fort, and very strong.

All the above forts are within two miles of each other, and flank the river, so as to render the passage of shipping almost impossible, and therefore accounts for the great land force which it has been deemed prudent to send. Lillo is distant from Antwerp ten miles.

Fort Shenis.—a secondary fort, but we believe a strong one. All the weaker forts having been demolished, none were left but such as were important by their local situation, or the artificial strength of their works.

Fort St. Philip's.—this fort has been demolished.

Fort St Boergarten.—a strong redoubt, very formidable.

Fort Biermanteli—in the immediate vicinity of Antwerp, flanking the river, and may be considered as one of the works of the city.

The several forts on the west bank of the Scheldt are of the same nature as those above described. The chief them of are Fort St. Anne, Fort Lies, Fort Lifenhoex, directly opposite Lillo; Fort Perle, and Callo.

You will be enabled to judge from this statement, what are our actual difficulties, and what is our final chance. I have before told you that there are already many long faces, and it begins to be confidently asserted that our success will terminate at Flushing.

I have just now heard a very singular character of the commandant of Flushing. His name is Monnet, and he has the reputation of being an able man; it is said, however, that he is cruel to a degree, and holds the poor Flushinger in the most sovereign contempt. So far, however, I can speak from my own knowledge, that the hardest part of the duty of sustaining the siege, is imposed upon these non-military Burgesses.

They are compelled, for they certainly do not officiate voluntarily, to discharge the cannon which are pointed against us; they are compelled to stand our fire; they are compelled to do the duty at the walls; and, if I am not mistaken, a great part of the slaughter committed by our shells, must fall upon them. In one branch of the service, indeed, they are not employed—they are not trusted in the sorties. These are made solely by the French troops, and, as I have said before, they are usually very brisk. The commandant has not risked his person in any one of these assaults upon our works; the second in command always leads them, and has displayed a vigour and a courage which have recommended him to our peculiar notice. There is something in courage which commands the regard of an enemy. I am persuaded that there is not a man in our lines who would willingly kill General Osten.

The garrison of Flushing is very well provisioned. The passage from Cadsand being open so long, enabled General Monnet to fill the garrison with stores of all kinds, The French soldiers, moreover, are less difficult in things of this kind than the British. This, indeed, is one of the characteristics of a French force. The consumption of an English body of men bears no proportion to that of a French body of equal numbers. The French can truly subsist on anything; whilst good living is so necessary to an Englishman, even to an Englishman of the lowest class, that they are no sooner put on short allowance, than even their courage, or at least their active spirits and vigorous enterprise give way.

You can scarcely imagine the vast effects which this difference produces in the results of a campaign. Whilst the English soldier is pining and drooping, and at length passes to the hospital, and thence to his grave, the Frenchman is as active as ever, and as merry as a beggar under a hedge. I have seen repeated instances of the truth of a maxim which I have before mentioned—that in the wear, and tear of a campaign, the French are infinitely superior to the English. The French hospitals are empty, whilst those of the English are overflowing.

The English motions and operations are impeded by their sick, whilst the French resemble so many weather-beaten gipsies; the rain runs off them as if it could not penetrate them, whilst the English are sensible at every pore. The English must have their warm bed and their sheltered lodging; whilst the Frenchman will sleep under, an hedge, and be contented with the shelter of a tree or bush and, to sum up all, a Frenchman will find food where an Englishman would starve.

I am sorry to have to inform you that the people of Middleburg have begun to imitate the people of Ramsgate, and, finding a good company of us here, have raised the price of every article of life to nearly double its former amount. I hope that this extortion will not be suffered to continue. It will be carrying our lenity too far, to allow them thus to abuse our indulgence.

You would be astonished at the flat insipidity, at the absolute insensibility of these Dutchmen; they regard us without any appearance of curiosity, and obey the orders which are given to them in the most submissive, but sullen silence. They say not a word either the one way or the other. The women even seem to have lost that curious nature which characterizes them in other countries.

Our vanity is not gratified by a single look which we can construe into admiration, or even into interest. They seem to consider us as necessary evils, and to bear with us as they do with their bad weather—give it a look to see how long it will last, and then walk in to smoke their pipes,

I believe I have already mentioned to you that, Lord Chatham passes almost the whole of his time in Middleburg, and that his residence there has given it the animation of a town of the first order. I really know not how to give you an adequate idea of the beauty of Middleburg. It is so fresh, so clean, so lively-looking, so many of its inhabitants are opulent in the first degree, and all of them so comfortable, that the very sight of the town infuses gaiety. A beggar is not to be found within its circuit. If all the towns in Holland are like this, the English towns will bear no comparison with them.

I am writing to you at a very late hour. Tomorrow is fixed for the bombardment by sea and by land. Congreve is preparing his rockets, and promising us the instantaneous destruction of the town. He is a very clever, active man, but his rockets are in more, favour with your Ministry than they are in the army. We scarcely consider them as fair; they are more destructive than useful.

They will certainly reduce a town to ashes; but humanity, and even policy, will teach us that this is purchasing it at a very dear rate. It should be in war as in civil engineering—they should be considered as the best workmen who can procure the requisite result at the cheapest rate. This sweeping destruction, this conquest by annihilation, is as inconsistent with prudence as with humanity. Such is the opinion of the military of Congreve and his rockets. When I say this, however, you must not understand me as objecting to the man. He is a, very worthy, humane, and efficient officer.

Orders have just been issued that the officers shall look with peculiar care to the health of their men. This has been much canvassed, and some have objected to it, as imposing a vexatious obligation, where there is already enough to fatigue and to harass, The best of our officers, however, are of a different opinion;

they agree that the best defence against the climate is the most minute attention to cleanliness. Farewell! We expect warm work tomorrow, and are already preparing for it.

Yours &c.

Letter 8

Lines before Flushing, August 16, 1809.
My Dear Friend,

I informed you in my last that we were upon the point of very warm work—the bombardment has begun and ended. Its effect was prodigious beyond all imagination. Lord Chatham viewed it from the streets of Middleburg, and is said repeatedly to have exclaimed, "What a noble spectacle!" It was indeed a noble spectacle, if the spectator could have banished from his mind all obtruding ideas of the misery which it must have caused.

The batteries were finished on Saturday night, the 12th, and on the following morning the ships were ordered to take their stations. By noon everything was completed. The batteries, according to all military opinion, were placed with great judgement, and their effect was in some degree anticipated from their position. Their principal force was on the right and centre.

The battery on the right consisted of thirteen twenty-four pounders, and six ten-inch mortars. The centre battery had ten twenty-four pounders, and two mortar batteries, the one of six ten-inch, the other of six four-inch. The batteries on the right bore directly on the left of the enemy, and enfiladed the sea-defences to the westward of the town; the guns in the centre enfiladed the enemy's left, and took their sea-defences in reverse. Between the fight and centre there was a battery of six twenty-four pounders, manned by the seamen, and also some ten-inch howitzers, which likewise enfiladed the enemy's defences. On the left was another battery of three twenty-four pounders, which bore on the right of the town. The mortar batteries were commanded by Captains, Adye, Macartney, and Fyers. Captain Monro commended the battery in the centre, and Captain Smith that on the right.

In confidence of the superior reach of his rockets, Congreve at last took his station behind all the above-mentioned batteries, and played off against the town in grand, style. According, however, to the report of the artillery officers, the colonel has been deceived in the opinion of the greater range of his arrows. In this report, however, there may certainly be something of professional jealousy. Congreve's rockets are an innovation on the established system, and therefore, as you may suppose, are not in great favour with those who have been regularly educated.

Everything being thus prepared, orders were issued for the commencement of the bombardment; and about two o'clock on Sunday both ships and batteries began to open upon the town. Nothing in nature, I think, could be more tremendous. The island shook as if under an earthquake, and every report of the cannon was followed by a most horrible crash. Bricks, timber, and splinters of wood flew about in every direction; and when the chimneys or any high point was struck, they were sometimes driven, almost whole, over the walls. The batteries were all so near, that the guns had their full force; they literally appeared as if they were tearing the city up from the roots.

The enemy at first made a brave shew of resistance, and several Dutch Burghers pointed the cannon manfully from the ramparts. The fire, however, soon became too hot for these peaceable citizens, and even for the garrison, and the town had an appearance as if we were playing on an heap of ruins. The walls fell in large fragments, the churches took fire, the houses fell in, and everything was shortly so involved in smoke, that the guns were aimed at random.

This horrible work continued the whole of Sunday afternoon and night. The town was repeatedly in flames, but the enemy continued their fire; gradually, however, this fire became less frequent; instead of volleys, it was reduced to single pieces, and instead of regular intervals, was at random. About ten o'clock on Monday morning Sir Richard Strachan got under weigh, and passing immediately under the sea-line of defence, poured in a most tremendous cannonade, and continuing in his station, repeated these dreadful broadsides for some hours. The brave garrison, for such they were still, stood to their gun; but the ruins now fell so thickly around them, as to bury even their guns.

The fire at length, therefore, necessarily ceased on the part of the enemy. There was still, however, no appearance of surrender; they obstinately kept up their colours when they could no longer fire a gun. I know no reason which should withhold us from doing justice to an enemy. The defence of Flushing was brave and military to a degree; and as long as I live, I shall feel a warm respect for General Osten, the second in command, to whom this gallant defence is imputed. It is to this obstinate bravery, to this honourable sense of duty in the officers, and this rigid obedience, resulting from good discipline, in the men, that the French owe their military superiority.

In more bodily strength and animal courage, three Frenchmen are not equal to two Englishmen or Austrians; but what they want in bodily frame, they compensate by their activity, their discipline, and above all, by their hardiness of composition. An Englishman on his gross flesh soon melts away under the fatigues of a campaign and the inclemencies of weather; whilst the skin and bone of a Frenchman repel the attack without suffering. The rain seems to run off him as if he was so much oilskin. This observation is forced on me by the weather in this island. There is not a man of us but has now his fever, his ague, or his cough; and if we stay here long, nine out of the dozen of us will be in our graves. The seamen seem to bear this climate much better than the soldiers. If Walcheren is to be retained as a permanent member of our empire, it will cost us 5,000 men in the year by sickness. You see that I have changed my opinion.

I have likewise changed my opinion in another point. I believe I have before mentioned that General Monnet, the commandant of Flushing, stood very high with us all, on account of the manful resistance which he opposed to our siege. I am sorry that I have to recant this declaration. Previous to the bombardment, a flag was sent to him, intimating that as the fire would be very heavy, our commander in chief would wish him to remove the women and children, and that they should have free access through our lines. General Monnet, consulting the prudence of assuming a lofty tone rather than the dictates of humanity, has sent an answer that he must decline our proposal, as he feels himself fully competent to defend the women and children himself. The inhumanity of this measure was aggravated by the absolute impossibility of the city holding out; but General Monnet was resolved, it seems, to act his part to the last. He seems to consider the Dutch as so many dogs.

General Osten, the second in command, is a very different man; he exposes himself in every sortie, and has been daily visible in the ramparts. You will ask why some of our marksmen have not picked him out. I can give you a probable answer, from a circumstance which I have frequently heard from the officers who have served in Spain.

When our soldiers have ever seen an enemy's officer fight with more than usual courage, they have almost invariably marked him out to spare him—"It is a pity to shoot so fine a fellow." How different is this conduct from that of the French, who as invariably aim their rifles at our best officers!

Another trait of a British soldier fell within my own knowledge. Seeing a fellow fire his musket as I thought without an aim, I asked him at what he was firing.

"Into the enemy's line."—

"Take aim at a certain object," said I; "fix on your man, and make that your, aim."

The fellow, however, still continued in his own way.

On my rebuking him sharply, he told me resolutely that his heart would not let him take a fixed aim at one certain man; "and it answers all the same purpose, Sir, to fire in the crowd."

Of the batteries which chiefly distinguished themselves in the bombardment, one of them, commanded by Captain Richardson, of the *Caesar*, astonished us all. It consisted of six twenty-four pounders, and played on the enemy incessantly. Every discharge seemed to be followed by a vast crash and ruin in the town. I must observe, by the way, that the seamen are all engineers, and manage the batteries as well, I had almost said better, than any of our artillery officers. They fire their batteries by broadsides, and the reports of the individual pieces ape seldom distinguishable. They always play, moreover, against a certain point till they have demolished it. I cannot, however, say that their aim is as exact as that of our engineers; but they certainty excel them in what I term the fire by broadsides. Their six-gun battery invariably went off as if only one gun.

The enemy's fire, as I have said continued very brisk till about ten o'clock on Monday, the 14th, when Sir Richard Strachan passed along their sea-line, and opening a destructive fire, brought down the town in masses. Lord Gardner followed Sir Richard; Sir Richard's ship grounded, and Lord Gardner's had the same fate. The whole army, being informed of the accident, were in terror for the consequences; but fortunately the town guns had been all silenced, and those immediately opposite the grounded ships, had been buried in the ruins of the felling rubbish. How fortunately does chance sometimes contrive for us

It was a part of the previous arrangements, that Sir Richard Strachan should have taken the same station the preceding day. Had he actually done so, and, grounded in the attempt, his ship would have been shattered to atoms. General Monnet had prepared a very large furnace for the heatings of balls red hot; a well-directed fire from our batteries had destroyed it on the 13th. Had this furnace and its correspondent battery been in existence, nothing could have saved the *Caesar* and the *St. Domingo*.

This horrible work, for such really was this bombardment, continued till about five o'clock in the afternoon of the 14th, when the fire of the enemy entirely ceased, and the commander in chief stopped it on our side. A summons was immediately sent into the town, to which General Monnet returned for answer, that he would reply as soon ail he had consulted a council of war. An hour was given him for this purpose; three hours, however, elapsed, and no answer was received.

It became necessary, therefore, to resume the bombardment;

and accordingly once more the ships and batteries began playing upon this devoted town. The fire was now more tremendous than before; because the rest of the men had given them new spirits. Congreve's rockets blazed about in horrible splendour. They are certainly more effectual than shells any dimensions.

The town was shortly on fire, and as seen through the darkness of the night, nothing could be more horrible or sublime. Imagine yourself within four hundred yards of a walled town—this town on fire in five or six parts—the flames raging amidst the darkness of the night—the cannons still thundering, and the walls, and chimneys, and roofs falling under the stroke of the balls, and you may have some faint idea of the dreadful scene which was presented to us. The interior of almost every house was visible; and when there was an interval of the noise of the cannon, it was filled up by the shrieks of the women from the city. Even the very dogs howled, and several owls and bats flew affrighted round the light.

I wish a painter had been present, that he might have preserved a scene unrivalled in sublimity. West would have produced a picture which would have amazed the world. It reminded me several times of the general tone and character of his *Death on the White Horse,* the noblest picture, at least to my thoughts, which the modern world can boast.

The bombardment continued in this manner till two o'clock in the morning, When General Monnet requested a suspension of arms for forty-eight hours. This request was refused, and two hours only granted. The bombardment then ceased; and Colonel Long and Captain Cockburn were sent to negotiate the terms.

The whole business was concluded in an hour, and the gates were put into our possession without the loss of a moment. As the Government dispatches will be sent off at the same time with this letter, I need not inform you of the articles. You will agree with me that the garrison merited them; and it has become the modern practice of war to reward valour even in an enemy. The garrison of Flushing have certainly done their duty; and had it not been for our ships, they would have held out six weeks longer.

About three hours before the surrender of the place, the army, or at least as much of it as was near the spot, was witness to one of the bravest assaults which have ever been made by British troops. Imagine a dark, gloomy, and almost tempestuous midnight, whilst the vault of heaven was rent by a most dreadful bombardment, and rockets, like meteors, hissed and blazed in the air. It was under such circumstances that Lieutenant-Colonel Pack, with a detachment of the 36th, 71st, and some of the German Legion, attacked one of the batteries of the enemy immediately under the walls, and carried it sword in hand.

All circumstances considered nothing could be more tremendous than this attack. From the darkness of the night, the men could scarcely perceive the mouths of the guns upon which they were marching. I know not whether I have ever before mentioned the extraordinary gallantry of the German Legion; there is not a regiment in our service which can excel these foreigners.

In every service of peril they have always been the first to volunteer; and it is equal justice to add that in the most dangerous services they have always conducted themselves with the most brilliant valour. I hope that their repeated proofs of the most heroic bravery will extinguish those remains of prejudice which the common people of England are but too apt to indulge against foreigners. Two or three such regiments as the German Legion would be of inestimable value in our service.

Nothing could present a more awful spectacle than the town as seen, by the morning light. I believe I have already mentioned that the walls are high, but the churches and houses very considerably overlook them. Imagine every house almost battered in, the churches on fire, and the interior rooms and walls of every house exposed to sight. The Dutch usually build their chimneys in a mass; all the chimneys of one, or even of two adjoining houses are built in an heap on the partition wall. Our shells and balls having struck them, had precipitated them on the roofs of the houses, which had broken down under the weight.

Congreve's rockets had thus found admission into the interior of the dwellings; and the fire of these arrows being very powerful and intense, the destruction they caused was frightful. It will not, I think, admit of a doubt but that in firing a town, these rockets cannot be equalled; and if it be a part of our established system, of warfare, as it is, to destroy as well as to take, this invention is certainly entitled to praise.

But I confess I think the objection against them to be good; they are more destructive than they are efficacious in compelling a surrender. They reduce a town by burning it to the ground; and should they ever pass into common use amongst belligerents, they would add to the mischief of war, without shortening its duration.

Our conquest of Flushing and Walcheren has not been executed without very serious losses. I should suppose, on a rough average, that it may have cost us, in killed and mortally wounded, about four hundred men.

Amongst these are some very valuable officers. Colonel Donaldson and Colonel Petot are neither of them expected to survive. Captain Brown is likewise very dangerously wounded, and poor Talbot, of the 5th Foot, is killed. The garrison of Flushing stood to their guns to the very last; they certainly defended the town to the utmost, and not a soldier amongst them but has merited the Legion of Honour.

The expectation of this reward must have a very powerful influence on the French army; and the justice, the exemplary impartiality with which it is distributed, must add to its effect. Accordingly, you may take this as an acknowledged truth, that, with the single exception of the English, the French soldiers, are the bravest in Europe.

They certainly give way rather quickly before the charge of our bayonets; but this must be imputed as much to the inferior strength of their bodies and their arms, as to our own superior courage. They are absolutely pushed back by the greater weight of the English column. These are, in fact, the main characteristics of the English and French armies. The French soldiers are very inferior to ours, but no military man will despise them.

I am sorry to say that there is some appearance of a different sentiment, and even of some asperities, between our commanders. Sir Richard Strachan, it is said, consider that much time has been unnecessarily lost, and that the very objects of the expedition have been, thereby endangered. But Sir Richard Strachan would do well to prove to us how Flushing could have been taken before. The weather has been miserable, and we had to land all the heavy artillery at Campveer, and to draw it nearly the whole breadth of the island to the lines.

The artillery horses were perfectly useless in this necessary service. The roads are so extremely narrow, and the ditches so numerous, that when the attempt was made, so many of the cannon were rendered useless by accidents, that it was resolved to give up the effort, and to drag them by men. When you add to this the heavy rains, and the muddy soil, you may easily form an adequate conception of the difficulty and fatigue of the first operations.

It is another very important point, moreover, that nothing could be done till the ships were brought round, so as both effectually to cut off the communication with Cadsand, and bear on the sea-front of the town. It is the opinion of almost every officer in the army, that Flushing would have held out six weeks, had it not been bombarded by sea.

The garrison was healthy and numerous, and the works were strong. Now the frigates were not brought round till the 11th. What would the naval commanders have? No time has certainly been lost in taking Flushing. The town certainly surrendered in two days after it was bombarded; but the bombardment was by sea and land. Any bombardment on the land-side would have been insufficient.

I have not as yet been in the town; no one is suffered to enter it without special permission. If Walcheren is to be permanently retained, I hope that Flushing will not be the head-quarters. Middleburg is superior to it in everything. This letter goes off with the Government dispatches.

Yours &c.

LETTER 9

August 18, 1809.
My Dear Sir,

I have just now returned from a walk through the streets of Flushing, and a more melancholy spectacle I have never beheld. Till the present day, it was prohibited to enter the town. Nothing is more laudable than the care which has been taken to prevent the soldiers from plundering the inhabitants. What you have heard of the discipline of our soldiers is true in the main; but there are some individuals in our regiments who would be better in your prisons. England, I believe, is the only kingdom in the world who transfers its thieves into the army. We feel the effect of this in every moment of hurry and confusion.

In the retreat, in the Spanish campaign, the laxity of discipline was so dangerous and so atrocious, as to compel Sir John Moore to notice it in his public dispatches. Straggling parties separated from the army, plundered every house, and maltreated every woman in their way. In our present expedition we have not as yet to make any complaint of this nature. But it is necessary to keep a strict eye and hand over some of our newly raised regiments. The Germans are an example of temperance and quiet deportment, and of attentive discipline; but I am sorry to say of the Irish, that they are as troublesome as they are brave.

It is impossible to walk through the streets of Flushing, from the mass of ruins which everywhere obstructs the way. The Burghers of every rank are employed in digging these smoking heaps, to search for the mangled bodies of their relations. Every moment some of these wounded frames are raised on biers, that they may be claimed by their relatives. These effects and appendages of war are truly horribly; it is necessity to invent it with gay apparel, to render her tolerable. The more I see the more do I become persuaded that nothing is so senseless as those objections to the gaiety of our dress, our music, &c. which you read in the military theorists. No one would become a soldier who saw war really as it is.

As to the extent of the ruin, about one third of the town is a mass of rubbish. Amongst this I am sorry to have to add, that all the public buildings are to be included. The *Stadt* House, as you may read in your gazetteers, was built on the model of that of Amsterdam; and as Flushing stands in a similar situation, that is to say, half under water, the resemblance was very complete.

It resembled it, however, more in its magnificent architecture than in the mere accidental point of situation; it was built according to Dutch industry, more solid than was necessary, but was altogether a most noble structure. Of this building nothing now remains but the outer walls; the fire has completely gutted it, and its roof and interior are all piled in one vast heap within the compass of its standing walls. It reminded me very forcibly of Drury Lane Theatre, but was in every respect a nobler building than that heavy mass of brick work.

One church has been completely burned to the ground; another was on fire several times; but the citizens, by the most incredible efforts, suppressed it, and saved their church. By all that I can hear, the Burghers conducted themselves during the siege with the greatest courage and coolness; they spared no efforts to save their houses; they extinguished the fuses with the most incomparable coolness.

The garrison, on the other hand, were perfectly negligent as to any consequences which might happen to the city. They compelled the Burghers, moreover, to man the works; and, if report may be believed, put them in advance. This indeed is the method which the French generally observe towards their auxiliaries. They push them in front, and then cut off their rear, so as to render their retreat impossible. The French officers never trust their foreign auxiliaries till they have placed them in a situation in which treachery or desertion would be impossible. The escape of Romana was a solitary instance.

Every house is perforated by at least one ball, and some of them by a dozen or more. Every roof bears evident proofs of the force and destructive extent of Congreve's rockets. It is almost wonderful to me that any of the women have been able to effect their escape. The stench of the unburied bodies is intolerable. Many of the women, during the bombardment, fled to the cellars, and fortunately none of the balls penetrated so far. There is a report in our camp that General Monnet pursued the same course; but as it is but a report, I shall give it no credit.

His conduct, as far as it has appeared to us, has been that of a very brave man; and it would be a pity that this character should be reported away. He certainly did not expose himself on the ramparts; but this is no part of the duty of a commandant. Lord Chatham himself was in Middleburg during the greater part of the siege, and yet no one thinks of imputing any blame to him. Why should we deal more hardly with General Monnet?

It is but justice, however, to add, that the garrison and the Burghers impute the destruction and reduction of the town to the bombardment by the ships. Such was the fury and the force of this fire, that the town would have been but one heap of ashes, had the bombardment not ceased when it did. About noon on Monday the whole town was enveloped in fire and smoke. The mortar batteries in the centre produced likewise a very powerful effect. It is reported that a shot from this battery fired the *Stadt* House. Captain Smith's batteries, however, rendered a still more important service:—the enemy had prepared a furnace for the purpose of heating red hot balls, and firing at the ships; but a shot from one of these batteries destroyed the furnace, and thereby saved the shipping.

I have already repeatedly mentioned the marine brigade, and the exemplary gallantry with which they performed every service committed to them. They managed their battery as if it was their ship—fired it by broadsides, and seemed to imagine the town a ship opposed to them. They fairly astonished our engineers by the correctness of their aim. I should hope that your *Gazette* will contain some merited mention of this brave corps.

The mischief of the siege has not been confined merely to the town; the sluices, as I have before mentioned, have been opened, and the whole country is under water. As Flushing lays low, the streets and lower apartments are flooded, and the only resource of the poor inhabitants is to live in the upper stories. Everyone blames the commandant for having recourse to this desperate measure; it has been productive of mischief which it will cost years to repair. The harvest is fortunately got in, or this mischief might have been yet more serious.

As it is, it has for the present spoiled all the water in the island, and flooded fields which will cost the utmost labour to drain. So much water, moreover; stagnating in the meadows, must necessarily corrupt the air, which is already sufficiently pestilent. Sickness has accordingly made an increasing ravage amongst us; some of the regiments have so seriously suffered, as to be declared unfit for duty. If the town had held out about ten days longer, the inundation would of itself have raised the siege. The bombardment was commenced exactly at the proper point of time; and fortunately one of the first operations was the acquisition of the battery which commanded the sluices.

The French garrison suffered very severely by the bombardment: but it is an established manoeuvre in the French army, to neglect no, means of concealing their killed and wounded. Accordingly the interval between the capitulation and the actual surrender was employed in burying their dead. The mode of this burial was very indecent. A pit was dug, and filled with bodies, when a slight covering of mould, about six inches thick, was thrown over them. Our soldiers in walking round the city, have stumbled upon one or two of these heaps. You may easily believe that such a stratum is not sufficient to confine the effluvia arising from so much corruption. Indeed it is not, and the air is infected beyond anything you can possibly imagine. There is pestilence almost in breathing it. I have been in the city once, and have had enough of it.

As to the numbers of the inhabitants who have suffered, it is not very easy to make an estimate. Every moment some mutilated body is dug from the ruins, and immediately put into a shell, and thence hurried to the common grave. The most respectable Burghers have fallen, and been buried in this indiscriminate manner.

We have just learned that on Sunday nearly one hundred of them were carried to their graves; and I am afraid that the bombardment of Monday must have been still more fatal to them. The French compelled them to bear all the brunt of the siege, to labour at the works, to share the peril, and to fire the guns. These poor fellows, unaccustomed to the trade and fatigues of such warfare, absolutely dropped under the unusual labour. The French contrived to station them so that retreat was impossible. The consequence was, that many of them perished from efforts above their powers.

As one proof of the comparative extent in which the Burghers suffered, I should not forget to mention that out of a battery which was served by twenty-two citizens, all perished but two. The French very ungenerously forced them into the most exposed situation. I should think that the French name will long be execrated in the Island of Walcheren.

One of your English newspapers have just reached me. I am perfectly astonished at the infamous calumny it contains. The passage is so circumstantially false, that I must give you the whole extract

> Nothing is more astonishing than the conduct of the army and the commander in chief before Flushing. Why does this town hold out so long? The public have much to complain of on this score. It is a general report in the English lines, that the town might have been taken by assault on the first night. The French prisoners admit their panic to have been so great when driven into the town, that they found it impossible to muster a single company, still less a regiment; and if any compassion be expressed for the fierce bombardment of the town before a Dutchman, it uniformly produces this observation—'Whose fault is it that the town suffers so much? Why did not your army come in at once, and then you would have taken possession of the town, without an hundredth part of the injury, and with one-third of the loss?'—Indeed it has been stated

that a proposition was made in the first instance to carry the town by assault; but that the proposal was declined, from a humane regard for the safety of the innocent inhabitants, who might fall victims to an assault.

Now every syllable of this is false. On the first night of our landing, a detachment of General Graham's brigade had a skirmish with the enemy on the Middleburg road, and followed them within cannon-shot of Flushing. But as to entering the gates, nothing could be so absurd as the assertion. Every house in Flushing would have proved a battery. It is really a disgrace to your free press, that it should thus sport with the reputation of the army. Any commander would have been mad who would have ventured thus to enter a city completely fortified: the assertion indeed almost conveys its falsehood in its absurdity.

Now I am upon this topic, I must not forget to mention that a great number of non-military visitors, under the pretext of belonging to the commissariat, have found admission into the island. Some of them are so troublesome and so prying, that measures I believe will be taken to repress this nuisance. We have already an English press established at Middleburg, and the first paper is to make its appearance on Saturday next. English boats are daily arriving, and there are evidently some preparations on an extensive scale for smuggling. The navy, I believe, are not very brisk in the duty of prevention. Nothing, in truth, is so difficult as to convince anyone but a custom-house officer that there is any criminality in smuggling. Seizure is accordingly considered as a species of direct robbery.

Immediately upon the surrender of the town, an important question arose what we were to do with the Burghers, who had manned the works, and carried on the whole of the siege against us. One opinion was in favour of treating them as prisoners; but it was at length determined to call them before a council of war, and examine them personally as to their motives. This was accordingly done; and it came out in their examination, that General Monnet had compelled them to take that active part, that they were pushed in advance, and all retreat and refusal cut off by a French guard behind. Upon learning this, Lord Chatham commanded them to deliver up their arms, and dismissed them in peace.

Every arrangement is making to put the town into a state of permanent defence. The enemy are evidently assembling in great strength in Cadsand; and there is a current report that the re-conquest of the island will be attempted. There is now a regular encampment immediately opposite to us in Cadsand; and Bernadotte has certainly arrived at Antwerp. You may imagine, therefore, that our labours have rather commenced than passed over. We have now, in fact, to repair all the mischief that we have done. The works must be restored to their original state. It would indeed be all over with the defence of Flushing, if the enemy could effect a landing before the town walls and batteries are put into some decent state.

General Picton, the former Governor of Trinidad, has been appointed Governor of Flushing. As a military character, the general stands high; but his reputation is not perfectly cleared up since the alleged transactions in Trinidad. His appointment therefore has excited some surprise, and perhaps some discontent. There were certainly many others whom the union of merit and long service should have entitled to a preference; but Picton is a ministerial favourite, and I am sorry to say that the army begins to feel a new kind of influence.

The French, it is said, are collecting gun-boats from Boulogne; they pass through the interior by canals, and may thus reach Cadsand, and the straight between us. You see, therefore, that if Flushing is to be kept, we must have an able force on the station.

From the Cadsand coast it is about two miles. The water is deep, and in a great degree secured from winds. The gun-boats therefore can be rowed over in despite of the utmost efforts of our ships. Such is the state of things as far as it respects the future defence of Flushing. Be the enemy's intentions what they may, the inhabitants of Flushing begin to apprehend another bombardment. General Picton accordingly has found it necessary to adopt nearly all the precautions which would be required were the town actually besieged. The sentinels are doubled every night; none of the inhabitants are permitted to come on the ramparts; no vessel, even British, is suffered to enter or leave the harbour without a passport; and the strictest regulations are enforced with respect to the arrival or departure of all persons not connected with the expedition. You would really be astonished at the crowd of spectators who have accompanied this expedition.

I have very little more to write to you upon the present occasion, except to repeat my lamentations on account of the dreadful sickness which is daily hurrying us to the grave by hundreds. It is a putrid intermittent, originating in cold and damp, and in bad air; the blood literally seems to stagnate, and to putrefy, because it cannot be put in motion. The same effect follows here from cold as in the West Indies from heat. The air is mortal. It is so thick as almost to choke you whilst you are breathing it. It is really impossible to enable you to form any adequate idea of the degree of this corruption. You may truly smell the air.

Middleburg, as I have said before, has the character of being comparatively healthy; but you might as well live in a well as in Flushing. Almost all our officers who were on duty during the siege, are now confined to their beds, and happy are they who can procure a bed to sleep on. The sick are frequently seen without shelter or covering.

Never in my life have I witnessed so much misery and sickness in mass. Nothing, moreover, can be more unlucky than the state of the weather. Every half-hour it rains—a true cold winter rain; the sun then breaks out, and throws us all into a perspiration; this will continue about an hour when the heavens are again overclouded, and the cold rain recommences. The constitution of Hercules could not support such a climate. How little dependence is to be placed upon your geographers! I have just been reading Rusching's account of this island; he describes it as peculiarly healthy.—Heaven bless the man! To be sure, he is a German, and some parts of Walcheren may be equal to some parts of Germany.

General Mackenzie Fraser is reported to be very ill. I am very much mistaken, or we shall lose the bravest of our officers in this Expedition. Death in the field is so natural to a soldier, that we think little of it; but to die under this pestilence—to drop like birds in a long frost—this is truly miserable. However there is no help for it; and according to the proverb, I suppose we must see the end of it by patience.

I am sorry to say that there is too much appearance even of a dearth of provisions; I should hope, however, that this would be but temporary. The harvest has been plentiful to a degree, and the sluices did not operate till it was got in. The wheat, moreover, is of a singularly good quality.

Of meat we must expect little, except what we receive from home; our numbers are too great to be supplied by the mere produce of the island. The Dutch inhabitants, moreover, are resolved to make us pay for whatever we use; prices are all doubled and trebled; and if we are to be supplied by the bakers of the island, something in the nature of an assize will be necessary.

I expect that you will inform me what is the public opinion of our operations in England. I should hope that your Opposition Papers are not the echo of it. They seem to be both bitter and unjust.

Yours truly

Letter 10

Aug. 20, 1809.

My Dear Sir,

I have just returned from a foraging party, which penetrated almost to Lillo. We were out two days, and our proceedings were not without some interest and importance. You can scarcely imagine with what spirit our men volunteer upon this occasion. A scooting or foraging party is always a party of pleasure; the danger, however, is very great, as well from the enemy as the enraged peasantry. The enemy are very alert in their defence; and the peasantry, if they see our approach from a distance, get behind the trees and hedges, and fire upon us like so many wild ducks.

Our loss of men, therefore, in these parties is very considerable, and would be much greater, but for the infinite superiority of our horses; the horses of the enemy are like so many animated skeletons compared to ours. We fairly ride them down whenever they venture to oppose us. English cavalry and English bayonets against the world!

From Middleburg we passed over to Beveland, and from Beveland to the bank of the East Scheldt, I believe I have before had occasion to mention that Beveland will not bear any comparison with Walcheren; Beveland is everywhere as flat as a table, whilst Walcheren is not without some elevations. Walcheren, moreover, being better cultivated, is better drained; in Walcheren there are some corn-fields, and many most beautiful meadows. On the other hand, in Beveland the meadows are almost all marshes, and there is scarcely any dry land but the roads. The roads, moreover, are as narrow as those in Devonshire, where it is necessary to use horses with panniers instead of carts. The Dutch have no idea of land-carriage; their roads are therefore little better than so many foot-walks.

The scenery of South Beveland, however, is not without some pleasing objects; it is new at least to a foreigner, and therefore pleases. The roads being somewhat elevated above the adjoining ground, give a good prospect over the fields which border them. From the abundance of moisture, the verdure of the meadows is incomparable; and when the weather is fine, you have a truly rich Flemish scene. The fields are covered with cattle in a proportion infinitely beyond what is usual on the same space in England.

If I mistake not, the English farmers feed at the rate of two large head of cattle per acre; the Dutch farmers extend this allowance to six or seven, and the cattle are still so fat and sleek, as to prove that the land is not overstocked. A Lincolnshire farmer would see this Flemish fertility with surprise. Ireland at present supplies the best part of the consumption of the Navy; if Walcheren be kept, we might put her under a similar contribution. The cattle is large, and usually very fat. If the grass were cut for hay, its burthen must be very great. Such meadows are, very rare in England.

There are two kinds of farmhouses in the islands of Zealand; the one so exactly resembling an English farmhouse, as not to merit any detailed description. The fashion indeed of this kind of house is very ancient; there is a porch which juts out from the centre, the inner pavement of which is raised. From this porch the house is entered by an immense oak door, thickly studded with nails; this opens into a narrow passage, on each side of which are the rooms of the house. The kitchen is floored with bricks; the ceilings covered with racks, and the sides with shelves and dressers; the fireplace is in an huge chimney, the hearth of which is considerably raised beyond the floor of the room. The main distinction beyond the English farmhouses in these kind of buildings is, that the ceiling is seldom plastered. It almost always consists of the rough beams, and which are of such density and solidity as to satisfy everyone that they were built in times when there was no scarcity of timber.

The other kind of farmhouse is peculiarly Flemish. It is little more than an immense barn, with its gable end turned towards the street or road, and in which gable end are the vast folding-doors. The inner part of this house is divided into two compartments, separated only by a boarding about three feet high. In the one part eat, drink, and sleep the family; in the other the cattle are all housed in the night. On the further gable end another door opens, and conducts into the farmyard, at the opposite extremity of which is the barn.

Nothing can be more simple, and, as I should think, nothing more uncomfortable than these habitations; but a Dutchman, both at home and abroad, has but one object in view—the accumulation of money. To this he most cheerfully sacrifices every comfort, happy if the present sacrifice, however great, can conduce to any future profit, however small.

In one thing alone a wealthy Dutch farmer resembles an English one; both Dutchman and Englishman go well-dressed. The Dutchman, on a Sunday, exactly corresponds with our idea of a Burgomaster; his wife, moreover, dresses equally substantially and comfortably. There is certainly such a thing as a distinct national character. The Dutchman is truly an original—as grave and sedate, but not as dull and melancholy as the Spaniard. Amidst all his gravity, a Dutchman has an air of content. He has no appearance of sullenness; he is silent without a contempt of others, and reserved only for his own ease. If you can make him a friend, he is a very valuable one. His fortune and his life are at your disposal. England does not excel Holland in instances of this magnanimity in domestic life.

The well-known story in the *Spectator* happened in Holland. Every woman in a besieged town was allowed to bring out with her whatever she valued most, and would carry on her back. The Dutch women availed themselves of the article, and brought out their husbands upon their shoulders. The English ladies would have done the same; but I would not extend this assertion to any other people.

The general condition of the Dutch farmers seems to be that, for the most part, they are as wealthy as the wealthiest class of farmers in England; but they have not the same ideas of comfort. A rich English farmer (I do not speak of that mixed race, termed gentlemen farmers) is always well-clothed, well-lodged, and well-fed; his table is not merely loaded; the articles which compose it, are of a good and substantial kind.

On the other hand, the table of a Dutch farmer has more vegetables than meat. There is a complete *farrago* of everything which the field and garden produce; potatoes, French beans, and cabbage are all hashed up, and very small, together; and two slices of bacon are added, to give them a relish. From this mess all the family feed with wooden spoons.

Everything in a Dutchman's house is for show, and not for use. The shelves, perhaps, are bending beneath a weight of pewter, and the cupboards beneath the heaped tankards of silver, whilst everything on the table is beggarly in the extreme. But if the pewter and silver were used, it might wear; and therefore for year after year it remains in the same place. No alteration is made in this custom, but when some branch of the family is married; the silver and pewter are then displayed in the best possible order, and the table of a Dutch Burgomaster would be a fortune to a German prince.

The Dutch husbandry is much neater, and in many respects more intelligent than even the English system. Their meadows are kept with garden neatness. No weeds are suffered to occupy the place of grass. The bye-paths which cross the fields, are kept as elegant as if they were so many garden walks. The hedge-rows are dressed with equal care. The slovenly carelessness of the English farmer, who, suffers every species of weed to mix with every species of grass, has no example here: the Dutch former never walks his fields without his weeding-hook, and every weed is removed as soon as seen. In Lincolnshire there are repeated instances of a whole dairy of cows being poisoned, and bursting, by swallowing some, of these pernicious plants; in Walcheren and the Bevelands there is nothing of the kind. A child poisoned would not cause a greater clamour, than a cow or heifer thus heedlessly lost.

As to the costume of these Dutch *boors*, it is between the English and Spanish. They usually wear an immense hat, almost as broad and large as the parasol of an English lady. We may here see the force of imitation, and the power of long habit. The Spaniards very naturally adopted these hats, from the nature of their country; a hot southern climate, where the noonday would almost level a man to the ground. The Dutch, whilst under the dominion of the Spaniards, adopted their customs without any reference to their origin; for surely, of all places in the world, Holland is one where there is least to fear from the ardour of the sun; and having once adopted them, they keep them up.

The remaining part of the dress of a Dutch *boor* is a doublet, and an immense pair of breeches. The doublet has the flap-pockets of a waistcoat; the breast of it is full of buttons, which are usually of silver, and which have passed from father to son, and from waistcoat to waistcoat in long succession. The Dutch coat resembles the shepherd's long coat of the north of England. To say all in a word, the ancient pictures of the Flemish School give you a very exact idea of the present Dutch costume.

There are several traits in the external character of a Dutchman, if I may so call it, which so nearly resemble those of an Englishman, that I cannot pass them over without notice.

In the course of our foraging party, we were necessarily compelled to ride over the fields, in some of which the harvest was yet uncut. This act of necessity provoked the most virulent abuse from such of the Dutch farmers as saw us. I have no doubt but that this abuse was conveyed in the worst possible language: we could understand it no farther than it was interpreted by their gestures. Every nation has a way of scolding peculiar to itself. In England they swear, in France they gesticulate; in Italy they scream; in Holland they stand stock still, and abuse with the most tranquil invective.

We passed many women, some of them weeding in the fields, others seeming to have no other occupation but to walk. Our general observation upon them was, that they were not so handsome as our own countrywomen. They had the most abominably thick legs and ankles, and for the most part fat, large faces. Their features, however, were not worse; they were feminine and soft. There was not one of them who would have been reckoned pretty in an English, village; but when you looked steadily in their faces, they were not unpleasing. The chief defect was animation, of which they have nothing. I should imagine, however, that, to compensate for this, they make very quiet wives.

The dress of the women is very ill calculated to repair any deficiency of personal charms. Their hats are as large as those of the men; they have a border in front of their gowns, and their stays are so stiff and so long, that they look as if planked up, from an apprehension of broken backs. An English female peasant in the old pictures is no imperfect representation of what the Dutch women are at present; young and old, they are all antiques alike.

We passed our night in a barn. Arriving at a late hour at a

farmhouse in a field, we knocked up the inhabitants. The old gentleman put forth his head from a wooden window, or rather wicket. Seeing so many soldiers, he drew himself hastily in, and shut the window. We repeated our knocks; he at length reopened the window, and as well as he could render himself intelligible by nods, informed us that he would come down to us. We were accordingly soon admitted, and made our beds on the floor. I must not forget to mention, in justice to Dutch hospitality, that he produced, unasked some bottles of mead.

Indeed the Dutch *boors* seem alike hospitable both to friend and foe; in this, respect they make no difference between the French and English, To be dry or hungry—to be a stranger, seems a sufficient recommendation. This part of their character delighted me still more, as it was so wholly unexpected, I had heard from every quarter where I had made the enquiry, that the Dutch were sullen and selfish, and considered everyone in want, as a nuisance. This is not just; the Dutch are as hospitable as the English.

You would be astonished at the immense number of wildfowl with which this island is covered—I speak of Beveland. When the weather is cold, they start up in every ditch; they fly strong, and are excellent in their kind. We have not time to employ ourselves in sporting, or I have no doubt that; we should live plentifully,

There is one singularity which strikes us strongly in passing along the Dutch roads; there are none of those carts, wagons, and coaches which are common even in the bye-roads in England. Everything is carried by water, and canals are everywhere substituted instead of roads. I have understood from those who have been in China, as far at least as is possible to any European to penetrate, that China is distinguished by the same peculiarity; every town having a canal, and these canals under the same regulations as roads in other countries. In Zealand and in China this arises from the same state of circumstances in both countries.

Both in Holland and in China, the surface is almost everywhere a dead level, and the soil so wet and marshy, that canals are easier made than roads. In both countries, moreover, it answer a double purpose; it drains the land, and renders it more fit for culture. From this abundance of canals, the land between them is firm and dry. In summer, indeed, the waters emit a most intolerable stench; the exhalations are pestilential, and from their density, are almost palpable. In autumn, when the weather is fine, and there is wind enough to agitate the water, the canals are covered with pleasure boats, the roofs and the cabins of which are full of people of all ages.

The phlegmatic character of the Dutch is visible in their pleasures. A Dutchman, in the plenitude of enjoyment, is fixed like a statue. No one would form any other judgement of him than that he was asleep with his eyes open. Where a Frenchman would be mad, and even an Englishman would forget himself, the Dutchman is fixed like a philosopher; immovably wrapped up in himself, and apparently enjoying the sunshine within.

Some of the Dutch gardens are peculiarly beautiful. They usually run back on the canals, and are thickly shaded with trees. In that part of them which borders upon the water, a mound is usually erected, covered with green turf, and where it is large enough, with flowering shrubs. On the summit is erected a summer-house of very grotesque architecture; it consists of two chambers, the one above, the other below.

The upper one is the constant sitting apartment of the better class of the Dutch families. Here they take their coffee in the evening, and look out at the boats which pass along the canals. I can assure you that by what I have seen myself, the Dutch do not seem to want suitable ideas of comfort. They have certainly not the levity of the Frenchmen, nor the elegant take which the general distribution of wealth has introduced into England. The Dutch of Walcheren and the Bevelands have almost all of them made their fortunes either by fishery or smuggling: the habits of these employments are certainly not very well calculated to form a good taste.

The effect of these early pursuits are sometimes ludicrously conspicuous. In every part of their garden are naval figures and appendages; Neptune waves his trident over a bed of cabbages, and a ship may be seen in full sail in a sea of parsley. Every tree taller than usual, is rendered at mast by rope-ladders; and the boys are very early taught this part of navigation, by manoeuvring up and down the apple or cherry-tree. You would be surprised to see the united agility and gravity with which these urchins run up and down the perpendicular pole which is erected for that purpose. The Dutch seem to have the same natural aptitude for the sea, with which foreigners have characterized the English.

I have repeatedly mentioned to you that the Dutch inhabitants of Walcheren and the Bevelands do not seem inclined to co-operate in our invasion. The state of their sentiments seems to be, that they wish to remain as they are, rather than incur new perils in an attempt, to improve their condition. If suffered to act according to their inclinations. I am persuaded that they would remain neutral, whilst England and France fought the battle out. I can compare the contest to nothing else but that of a lion and tiger fighting astride the carcase of another. Holland seems to have resolved upon submission; and therefore the present master is better than any future one, because to exchange her servitude, she must necessarily encounter the evils of a new struggle. With these sentiments, I do not think that we have much to expect from Dutch cooperation.

I am sorry to have to add a very unpleasant point of intelligence—that there is not the best possible understanding between Sir R. Strachan and Earl Chatham. It is currently reported that Sir Richard imputes to the Earl a very unnecessary delay in the operations of the expedition. The land officers, however, almost to a man, take the part of their commander; and I am one of those who think that everything has been done which could have been expected.

But so much I must say, that the expedition was certainly sent upon bad information. Whence does it happen that we are thus grossly deceived in essentials? Is it that we are too credulous, or that the frauds practised upon us exceed the ordinary degree and measure. If your cabinet at home had been thoroughly informed of the scene of operations, they would never have sent such an expedition, and certainly would not have so appointed it in artillery and cavalry. The carriages of our artillery are too broad, and our cavalry is here literally useless.

We penetrated so far as to have an immediate view of Bergen-op-Zoom; the garrison, however, took the alarm, and we were compelled to make a speedy retreat. It is but fair to acknowledge that the speed of our horses was here very useful to us. The French cavalry horses are perfect vermin. They would not be accented for an hackney-coach in London. The Flemish horses are very good; but they are very heavy, and want animation. The French cavalry are very far behind their infantry. I am perfectly astonished when I read of their victories over the Austrians in Italy; the German horse are so infinitely superior to them in weight, and in every military quality, that it is really inconceivable to me how the battle of Marengo, as stated in the bulletins, could have been gained by the French horse.

I am sorry likewise to add another unpleasant point of intelligence, which is that there is every reason to believe that our expedition is finished. The enemy have become so numerous, and have taken such strong stations, that it is the opinion of all our engineers that they are beyond our reach. Fort Lillo is surrounded by marshes, and on the land side is only approachable by a causeway, which by intersections and trenches may be rendered impassable. The ships are already below Lillo, and if they lighten themselves, may get even below Antwerp. Nothing therefore is to be done unless we can take both Lillo and Antwerp. As to Lillo, it will certainly stand a siege: and it is an important question whether, in the present state of things, we can afford a siege. Farewell! We are not in the best spirits, as the weather is bad, and our military prospects not very promising.

Yours &c.

Letter 11

August 26, 1809.
My Dear Friend,

Everything remains so precisely in its former state as to our military prospects, that I have very little to add to what I have formerly written. Of one thing I begin to be persuaded, that we shall stop where we are. The French are becoming very strong on both sides the Scheldt and information has just reached us that our flotilla have not deemed it safe to approach Fort Lillo. In the meantime we have councils upon councils; but nothing is as yet resolved upon, Congreve, who is in high favour with Lord Castlereagh, is sent home to explain the present state of affairs.

To give you my opinion fairly, we shall not be three weeks longer in Walcheren. It does not in any way suit the constitutions of our men. You would think that the rot was amongst them, were you to see how they drop off. Every hour three or four of them are announced to have departed, and some of the battalions are already skeletons. The men, moreover, become panic-struck; and whenever this happens in an army, or indeed in any multitude, the most harmless disease becomes contagious and fatal. We really begin to present a very different figure from what we were when we left England.

Our Commissariat business is very strangely managed. In this wet country everything depends upon being warmly and drily clad. There is a miserable deficiency of everything that is necessary to this purpose. We have no flannels or blankets; even our shoes are so execrable as not to exclude the wet; the leather is like so much brown paper, and tears off the sole after it has got one of two wettings. These are our contract shoes. Why is not care taken by the proper Boards or Commissioners that these shoes are sufficient for their purpose? It is incredible what a loss the public sustains by this culpable neglect.

No contractor should, be trusted in a business of this nature. There is not one of the numerous manufactured articles which are supplied to an army by contract, that is of a standard goodness. Everyone thinks that he has a clear right to cheat Government. In the meantime the poor soldiers suffer for all. You would really pity us if you saw the miserable figures to which the wants of these essential articles have reduced us. Many of our poor fellows are actually in the last stage of sickness without common necessaries. Should not this become the subject of serious enquiry?

There is one want, however, which is still more serious than that of clothing: the medical department complain of a want of bark. It seems that this is the specific for the diseases of the country. We have brought very little with us, and none is to be procured. The shops of Middleburg are almost totally without it. You know that I have always reprobated that foolish law by which bark was declared contraband of war, under the apprehension that neutrals might supply the enemy with it.

This law was as nugatory as it was cruel. It was nugatory, because it in no way promoted the main end of the war—the subjection of the enemy; and it was cruel, because it affected that part of the enemy which all civilized nations concur in pitying and relieving.

The sick and wounded are surely not proper objects of hostility. But at the time of this law, our Government was mad. The orders of council against America were part of the same system. Because France could not execute her own decree, we must retaliate, as we called it, by taking the execution into our own hands.

You may imagine that in our present state of inactivity, we are not objects of much dread or respect to the Dutchmen of the island. Every eye seems to enquire of us what we are about, what we shall do with Walcheren, and what is our further purpose? These are questions which I will not attempt to answer; the commander in chief himself seems to be in a maze.

Since Flushing has been taken, the quarters of the officers have been much improved; but I am sorry to have to add that the poor soldiers are not a whit better than before. All the streets of Flushing and all the lower apartments of the houses; are inundated to the depth of three or four feet; the consequence is, that the inhabitants are compelled to live in the upper rooms: the capacity of the town is thus much diminished. Add to this, that our commanders in this respect are much more moderate and indulgent to the inhabitants than are the French under similar circumstances. When Junot seized upon Lisbon, he suffered all his officers not only to choose their own quarter but to distribute the soldiers amongst the best houses. If there were room enough both for the inhabitants and for their new lodgers, it was all very well; if not, the proprietors turned out, and the lodgers succeeded them.

The practice of the English commanders is directly the contrary. The soldiers are punished even capitally for the slightest trespass attended with violence; and the property of the inhabitants is infinitely more respected and secure than under the former Government. It is only to be wished that they were more sensible of this favour.

Whilst everything amongst our general officers is confusion, deliberation, and apparently no ultimate arrangement, we of humble rank live in great ease, and, to say the truth, in great comfort. The citizens of Middleburg have become as it were accustomed to us; it indeed seems to be one of the characteristics of a Dutchman that he soon reconciles himself to everything. Entertainments; are daily given, and the officers are invited. The ladies moreover, have, become conciliated; and if we could but understand their language, our time might pass pleasantly enough. Fortunately their features are more intelligible; and if any of us pushed for a Dutch wife, I am persuaded that we should not have much difficulty in procuring one.

Middleburg is Amsterdam in miniature; it contains, on a smaller scale, whatever may be seen at Amsterdam on a larger. Amongst either Dutch institution, the one I most approve is their marine education. Every town has a naval asylum supported by Government. Here the children of the Burghers, and indeed of all Dutchmen, of whatever class, are educated at the public expense. They are received at seven, and retained till eleven or fourteen years. A certain number of them are then sent into the merchant and public sea-service. Hereafter they are to form a kind of standing supply for the French navy. If any Continental nation can establish a marine, it is France; and unless England have an eye upon her, she will, before another war, have a fleet not inferior to our own. In all the yards of these marine schools, are brigs completely equipped for practical instruction.

The Houses of Correction in Holland are on a better and more systematic plan than in England. They are called Rasp-Houses. The gaol of Middleburg does not merit any particular description, and has very seldom, I believe, even a single inhabitant. One part of all these buildings is the warehouse for the stock and manufacture of the prisoners. Every prison has a yard; but the space is usually almost filled up by piles of wood, which the criminals are employed in rasping. In one corner of the yard is a whipping-post.

The ordinary punishment of theft is, that the criminal is sentenced during a certain period to rasp or saw for the public service. The wood which they rasp, is log-wood; the wood which they have to saw, is campeachy wood. The labour of sawing or rasping is at first very great; but they become gradually accustomed to it, and the difficulty then, ceases. A certain quantity is required of each prisoner. Another peculiarity is, that the prisoners have a prison dress, which is furnished them at the public expense. Should not this be imitated in England? Can anything be more miserable than the appearance of the unhappy persons in an English prison? If reformation be sought as well as punishment, the comfort and compelled cleanliness of the criminals would certainly conduce to it. The first step to reform is to instruct a man to put some value upon himself.

The Dutch Workhouses are likewise worthy of peculiar attention. There is one of them in Middleburg. It is a large building, and is admirably contrived for its double purpose, the relief of objects really distressed, and the salutary correction of the idle and dissolute poor. This building is usually better inhabited than the gaols, as the Dutch magistrates seem naturally inclined to lenity, and seldom send those to gaols who may be reformed by a moderate correction in a workhouse.

These workhouses, however, are of more extensive use than in England. They are employed as a kind of family police. If a wife be troublesome by her temper, or even by her extravagance, the husband may complain to the magistrates, and upon proving his case, procure an order for the commitment of his wife for any time he may require. For this convenience, however, he is compelled to pay according to the rate of himself and his wife. The woman is treated according to her offence, with very little reference as to her situation in life. If her tongue had been too active for the quiet of her husband, she is put under a strict discipline of silence and quiet. If she were extravagant, she is compelled to assist in the household economy of the workhouse, and to live on the prison fare. What would your English ladies think of such an institution in England?

Neither are wives the only part of a Dutchman's family who may look with terror upon the town workhouse. In every large Dutch prison, one range of buildings is set apart for refractory daughters and disobedient sons. Whoever may happen to have undutiful children, may send them here. These genteel prisoners, for there are many of them of the first rank and fortune, are kept apart by themselves; they are compelled, however, to wear a certain dress, and to do certain stated tasks. If they fail, or if they misbehave, they are manually corrected by certain persons appointed for that purpose. The Dutch, in a word, seem to have overlooked nothing which may be necessary to their domestic peace; they have passed everything over to the care of the Government, and they have a kind of domestic connection with the prisons and the workhouses.

I am happy, however, to be enabled to add, that the greatest precautions are taken lest this power should be abused, and that in certain flagrant cases *Mynheer*, the husband, may himself be sent there upon complaint of his wife. Adultery is never overlooked either in man or woman; either of them may complain of the other, and a most severe punishment follows upon conviction. As far as my own observation goes, I can almost take upon myself to state, that the Dutch wives rule their husbands with a rod of iron; and whatever may be the pride, the obstinacy, and immobility of *Mynheer*, he seems to move briskly enough under the summons or the apprehension of his wife. The Dutch women are excellent house-wives, and, with the most patient looks in the world, are always in a bustle. Some of them, as I have said, are very handsome in the face, but almost all of them have legs most abominably thick; and after they have been wives for a year or two, lose all symmetry of shape and figure.

The general characteristic of the Dutch ladies seems to be, that they are the best housewives in the world; to this they sacrifice all their time, and this is their sole ambition. They all of them, however, have a certain degree of education; they can speak French, and even write German. Their deportment very nearly resembles that of the English. They express a dislike of the French manners, and never imitate them. Their decorum and evident modesty impress even a military visitant with respect, whilst their simplicity speaks forcibly to the heart. In the unmarried state they are without prudery, and in the married they have the reputation, and I believe very deservedly, of being examples of conjugal fidelity, They are more fond of dancing than anyone would anticipate from their apparent gravity; they dance more in the English than in the French style, and many of their dances are exact counterparts of our favourite English country dances.

Middleburg, as I believe I have before mentioned, has some very handsome houses; they are very high, and both internally and externally very clean. In the good houses the furniture and economy is more French than English, and every house is well furnished. The sides of the rooms are usually painted in landscapes; there are few of them merit *stucco* or paper. Every house, moreover, has some picture of value; and I have no doubt but that a good judge might make some very valuable discoveries of the works of the Flemish masters in houses which are, however, little expected to contain such a treasure.

It is not very easy to obtain any information as to the details of domestic economy in a Dutch family. I have endeavoured, however, to make out a list of the present prices of the most material articles of Dutch housekeeping; the result is, that housekeeping appears to be at least one-half cheaper than in London.

A good house in Middleburg is about sixty pounds *per annum*, such a house as would be at least two hundred in London. The taxes are comparatively nothing. The usual dinner hour of the upper classes is about three o'clock; the number of servants is not so numerous as is usual in similar establishments in England, and wages are infinitely less. It must not, however, be denied that the domestic establishment has not the same splendour, nor the same completeness as in London. The servants are without liveries, and none of them seem to know their business. They merely obey the word of their master, but seem to have no idea of anticipating it.

The greatest inconvenience in Middleburg, to a stranger at least, is the miserable state of the water; not even the common people can drink it. There is accordingly a trade here unknown in any other town in Europe, except it be at Madrid. There are water merchants, who import water from Germany, and in this trade employ a very large capital. Some of these vessels go as far as Utrecht in Germany, and bring a lading of stone bottles with water. These bottles are sold at about sixpence English. Fuel is another article which is rather dear; with the exception of wood and water, every other article of life is nearly two-thirds cheaper than in England; and one hundred pounds *per annum* would go as far as three or four in London. Poultry of all kinds is very cheap; and before the arrival of the English, was very plentiful. Butter is likewise infinitely cheaper than in England.

There is one peculiarity at the table of a Dutchman—you find no port wine; Claret is universally substituted. This is the more extraordinary, as the superior strength and body of Port wine are certainly better adapted to the climate than Claret. The Claret, however, is very good; not that wretched stuff which you drink so plentifully in Ireland. Claret is cheaper here than cider in England.

The Dutch Trade Laws, many of them at least, might be incorporated with those of England to much advantage. The laws respecting debt are the disgrace of England; in Holland they are mild to a degree: yet are commercial interests as much attended to in Holland as in England. No citizen is subject to arrest in mesne process. The method of proceeding against him is by summons; and this is repeated three several times, by which the debtor obtains about a month to settle with his creditor; if this settlement be not made, the debtor is arrested at the expiration of the last summons. This arrest, however, must not be made in a dwelling-house in every part of Holland a Dutchman's house is truly his castle. Should not this maxim be adopted in England? The Bankrupt Laws of Holland are more severe than those of England; every creditor must sign the certificate before it be allowed. If the debtor, however, be detained in prison, the creditor is compelled to make him a very liberal allowance.

The canals in Middleburg and Flushing are almost as dangerous to health as they are convenient for commercial purposes. Every offal, and all rubbish of every kind, is thrown into them; their surface accordingly resembles that of a horse-pond; and under a hot sun, they are impure and offensive to a degree. Scavengers are indeed in daily pay to keep them clean; but their ideas of cleanliness seem to be on a level with those of their masters. Once every year the canals are emptied of their mud, which is sold to the farmers, and which is a most valuable manure. It is impossible but that these impurities must be very dangerous to the health of the inhabitants. Habit, however, is everything; and the Dutch, from being daily accustomed to their sweet odours, seem neither to think of them, nor to be sensible of them. The depth of these canals is usually about eight feet. The sediment of mud at the bottom is at least of equal depth. An Englishman is almost poisoned by the exhalation before he becomes accustomed to it.

As this is a letter of scraps and patches, I shall put together everything which I have remarked characteristic of Dutch manners. I must not forget, therefore, the *carillons*, which are common in every town in Holland. These *carillons* answer to your English chimes: they are played by means of keys which are connected with the church bells. Nothing, however, in England can equal their perfection in Holland. A *carilloneur* as regularly belongs to every Dutch church as an organist to an English church. The tunes which the bells are thus made to produce, are sprightly and musical. They play at certain hours every day, and more particularly at noon and in the evening. The whole population of the towns then walk up and down to enjoy the harmony.

The labour of the *carilloneur* is so excessive, and so difficult, as to incapacitate him from any other business during the day. Nothing can be more delightful than this music when heard from a distance. In England the harsh and long pauses in the chimes take away from you all idea of harmony. In Holland the notes are made to run into each other as voluble as if they were those of a pianoforte. This is the more extraordinary, when it is considered that the force required to move the keys of the larger bells exceed some pounds in weight. The *carilloneurs*, however, are rendered so dexterous and attain so much strength of hand by long habit, that they can execute the most difficult pieces and even play in concert with other instruments.

An Englishman, indeed, finds this music somewhat monotonous; but when he remembers that it is produced by bells, he feels an agreeable surprise that they can be brought to such perfection. It is stated in some recent books of travel, "that the *carillons* at Amsterdam have three octaves, with all the semitones complete, on the manual, and two octaves on the pedals; each key for the natural sound projecting nearly a foot, and those of the flats and sharps, which are played several inches higher, only half as much."

Sir John Carr adds, that when the British army entered Alkmaar, they were agreeably surprised by hearing the church bells of that town strike up "God save the King!" In England such an event would have been an exhibition, which would; have invited the curiosity of a country.

All the churches in Holland are filled with the armorial insignia of the families which are there buried; and flags and shields from the earliest days of the States, are suspended in melancholy train from the roofs and walls. In the church of Middleburg are many of these sepulchral ensigns. I know not anything which, at first sight, so forcibly appeals to the imagination of the spectator. Conceive yourself, for example, to be walking through dark Gothic aisles, whilst these tattered remnants of former ages are quivering with the wind over your head. Would not your imagination immediately fly back to those early ages when, the heroes, of which these are the mementos, played their active parts on the stage of life?

These mighty men are now returned to the dust from whence their bodies were taken; and the reflection must forcibly press itself upon the mind of the spectator, that a very few years must pass before the same fate awaits himself. How truly miserable would be the condition of man unless he were assured of a future life! The horror of annihilation is of itself a very powerful argument that it is not suitable to our nature.

Have I mentioned to you, in any of my former letters, that the breach of chastity is very severely punished amongst the Dutch? Pleasure, however, sometimes misleads an unfortunate woman; a child is born before marriage, and the unhappy mother cannot conceal her disgrace. Her punishment under these circumstances, is to be sent into the solitary confinement of a place called the Spin-House, where she is compelled to do penance by working for the good of the State.

The Dutch endeavour to convert everything into active produce; and the greater of their punishments comprehend some contribution to the public stock. By these means they obtain two ends—correction and economy. The prisons not only pay themselves, but contribute something towards the revenue of the Government.

The general scenery in Walcheren by no means corresponds with what you would think it. Talk of Holland in England, and you are told of marshes and low lands, till you imagine it to be the most miserable region in the world. This is a very erroneous idea. The canals in the evening are enlivened by water parties, whilst the roads are covered with carriages as elegant as any of those you will see in London. Of course I am speaking of the prosperous times of peace. Even now, however, we are not totally without something of this gaiety.

The weather has been of late very unfavourable; but I have seen enough of the disposition of the inhabitants, to perceive that, under good masters, they are as well inclined towards pleasure as any people in the world. The Dutch girls look very demure; but I fancy that ways and means might be contrived to infuse a little animation into their minds and features. At present they look like so many Quakers.

The Dutch roads, as I have before informed you, are very much neglected; turnpikes, however, are as common in Walcheren as in Shropshire: but as the roads are but little used, they are narrow, and in bad weather impassable. We experienced this to our cost, in endeavouring to bring our artillery by horses from Campveer to the lines. We were compelled, after the most horrible fatigue, to give up the job, and to drag them by hand.

There is another peculiarity in Walcheren which very forcibly struck me this morning. (I write by fits and starts, and therefore without connection.) I allude to the very unhealthy appearance of all the children of the island. They exactly resemble the children of Europeans born in India. They have a deadly paleness, a kind of mother-of-pearl complexion, which must be seen before it can be well conceived.

Some travellers have imputed their sickly appearance to the peculiar method by which Dutch children are almost universally reared. This method is certainly bad enough in all conscience, consisting of a total exclusion of all air and motion. But the true cause seems to be the climate of the island, which, whatever the German geographers may have said of it, is certainly not favourable to population. I should think that half the infants who are born, must die before their fourth year.

I have resolved to throw together in this letter everything which has occurred to me of singular and characteristic. Our first impressions in a new country always attach to novelties, and these novelties are generally worthy of notice and observation.

The business of a Dutch undertaker is infinitely more comprehensive than that of an English one; he is compelled to have a certain number of servants habited in black, who are called Anspreekers. The office of these men is to enquire day after day as to the health of the undertaker's future customer; and as soon as the breath shall be out of his body, to carry the intelligence of it to all his friends and acquaintance. The costume of these melancholy messengers: consist of a black gown and band, with a craped hat. One would imagine that the common feelings of the people would abolish this custom. Surely there is sufficient misery in the world, without having the spectacle and appendages of death so constantly presented to our eyes.

The Dutch marriages are likewise very different from those contracts in England. When a young couple, and all the parties concerned, are agreed, a day of feast is appointed. When the company are all assembled, they follow the bride and bridegroom in procession to the Town House, where the contract being read, is signed in the presence of the magistrates, and confirmed by the authority of the law. From the Town House the happy assembly adjourn to the church, where the priest gives his benediction, and concludes the business.

I am happy to be enabled to say that, though this religious sanction of the civil contract be not required by the Dutch laws, it is never dispensed with by Dutch manners. This way of thinking leads them, no doubt, to a more serious consideration of the duties of that state. Another singularity prevails in a Dutch marriage. Where the friends and connections of the parties are too numerous to be invited to the nuptial dinner, a bottle of spiced wine, decorated with ribbons, is sent round. This seems to answer to our English bride's cake.

You will imagine that, from the numerous canals which intersect this island in every quarter, and which run up all the streets of the town, many accidents must happen. These, however, are not so frequent as would seem almost inevitable. The Dutch, though in a similar climate to our own, are infinitely more sober; a drunken man is a rare spectacle in Holland. It is the standing disgrace of the English Government that, for the sake of ,its revenue, it encourages, or at least does not repress, this beastly propensity of the lower classes. The frequency of public houses is the cause of the English national drunkenness. Every fellow feels himself dry when he passes a public house, and he will not repress his want when the means of gratifying it are so immediately at hand.

In Holland public houses are in no greater number than the public accommodation for lodging and travelling refreshment require. The town council is very careful that help shall be at hand in the event of any accidents in the canals. Similar printed bills for resuscitating the drowned are everywhere posted up, as in London; and rewards more liberal than in London, are conferred upon those who have been the happy instruments of saving the lives of their fellow-creatures. The English Humane Society, I believe, were indebted to the Dutch for their present process in the recovery of the drowned.

The trade of Middleburg before the war was very considerable; it consisted chiefly in the fishery which it had established on its coast. The cod and herrings taken were salted on the spot, and almost immediately exported to the Mediterranean. I know not whence it is that the Dutch have always excelled the English in this fishery, and in time of peace furnish almost the whole of the foreign market.

One cause would seem to be, because labour is cheaper in Holland than in England; and another, because there are no taxes upon salt. Some of our wise ministers, in hunting out a tax, very frequently fell upon the raw material, and immediately lay it under contribution, without any consideration that they are thus attacking the root and source of other taxation.

The Dutch, moreover, pickle and preserve their herrings in a manner very superior, to what is possessed by any other nation; the secret is said to be in salting the fish: I should think that it was rather in a careful sorting of them after they were salted, and when about to be packed. Be this as it, may, there is a secret, and though trusted to thousands, it has never been discovered. The persons employed, are sworn never to reveal their method of practice, and the oath has been kept as well as that of Masonry.

I am very happy to have to inform you that, from a liberal consideration of the Dutch poor, the English Government have given permission to the Dutch fishermen to continue their fishery as well in war as in peace. This was humane. It is not necessary to extend the evils of war beyond what the natural ends and object of war require; and no end or object could be answered by this persecution of fishermen.

We have set an example to France, which in principle, if not in this particular application, it is to be hoped that her rulers will follow. Nothing could be more cruel than the former practice, and more particularly as it was acted upon by the smaller privateers on both sides. If a fishing-boat was seen, it was universally scuttled and sunk, and two or more poor wretches thus reduced to the most abject poverty, their boats being their instrument of livelihood.

Middleburg, like many other principal towns in Holland, has specimens of almost every religion under the sun; and, from the toleration which is extended both by the express laws, and by the manners of the people, everyone lives in harmony with the other. Where this toleration is not synonymous with religious indifference, it is the happiest trait in national character.

Jews, the most unpleasant of all the race of men, because the most antisocial, abound in every town and hamlet in Walcheren; they are the only sect who do not intermix and visit. The Dutch Government do not merely protect them, but have cautiously endeavoured to remove those prejudices against them which their peculiar habits have excited. The Government, however, has been foiled in this attempt. It may render them tolerated, but it will never do more.

The clergy of the several religions, Catholics, Lutherans, and Jews, are all supported by their respective congregations or parishes. Each officiating minister has a certain fixed salary, and which is raised by rate on the parish to which he belongs. I could not obtain an answer to my question, how this was contrived in a parish where there were three or more different persuasions.

But I must proceed no further—Farewell!
Yours &c.

Letter 12

Middleburg, Aug. 27, 1809.
My Dear Friend,

The commander in chief, and the greater part of the army, have left the island for Beveland; and, from the present evident state of affairs, reports have been converted into, assertions that nothing farther will be attempted. If you will have my unbiased opinion, I will give it in a very few words. Too much has been done already. The expedition, as having been undertaken on insufficient grounds, and partial information, should be instantly abandoned. I hope that the false pride of appearing to have done something, will not induce your ministers to set an improper value on what has been done, and to act upon that false estimate. My decided opinion is that the sooner we return to England, the better. The following proclamations were issued on Monday last:—

Proclamation

His Excellency Lord Chatham, commanding the troops of his Britannic Majesty, being informed that many deserters, and persons belonging to the French troops, and some of them armed, are on the island, orders, that the before-mentioned armed or unarmed deserters, or other persons, be arrested, and delivered over to the nearest English detachment, and that no one presume to harbour such deserters, on pain of being sentenced, on conviction, to pay a penalty of 100 florins (one-half of which shall be given to the informer, whose name shall be kept secret), and be otherwise severely punished according to military law. Military deserters, and other persons belonging to the French army, not surrendering within three days, shall be punished as spies.

Proclamation

His Excellency Lord Chatham, &c. &c. being informed that many persons pass from one island to another, without being furnished with the necessary passports, orders, that no one presume to repair from the island of which he is an inhabitant, to another island, without having obtained a passport from the magistrate, which must be signed by the general, or commanding officer, on pain of being arrested.

All ferrymen and mariners are commanded to take no one over unfurnished with a pass. The transgressor of this command shall not only suffer the loss of the boat, or vessel, but shall, according to circumstances, be punished according to military law.

Nothing can be more frightful than the present condition of the part of our army in this island. It is distributed between Campveer, Middleburg, and Flushing. The two former towns are comparatively healthy, but Flushing is sickly even to a pestilential contagion. Our poor fellows are dying by companies. From twenty to thirty are buried every morning or night; and lest the frequency of these incidents should infuse a panic, the burials are before the rising or after the setting of the sun.

The order to this effect was founded on the fatal experience of the contrary in our West India islands. Instances have frequently occurred where, of those who have attended the burial of a comrade, everyone has been seized with a depression of spirits which has invariably proved fatal. In all these contagious diseases the power of imagination is wonderful. Imagine that you must die, and your death is certain.

It would be the extreme of ingratitude not to acknowledge the ability and the humanity of the physicians and surgeons; the medical department, without a. single exception, is very ably filled, and they have employed all the powers of medicine to stop the progress of this fatal disease. But the root of it cannot be successfully reached. It lies in the air we breathe—every inhalation is a putrid poison. The nerves are relaxed by the cold damp which obtains an entrance into the body, and the blood is corrupted by the putrid atoms.

The disease commences with every symptom of an ague, from whence it passes into a fever; and after the fever, the blood is putrefied. Livid spots break out on the arms, legs, &c. and the unhappy sufferer dies, when, in the absence of the fever, there appeared some hopes of his recovery. I know not whether the fatality of all new climates to Englishman, may not be imputed in a great degree to their former habit of living on such a quantity of animal food. Of all the foreigners in the English army, none of them suffer in any proportion to the English. The rot seems amongst us alone; and every ditch, every field, and every street are full of our dying and dead.

Sir Eyre Coote, who now commands in chief in Walcheren, has been over to Beveland to attend a Council of War. It is confidently asserted since his return to this island, that the decision of the Council has been, that further operations are impracticable; that the French have become too strong for a *coup-de-main,* and that our force is not sufficient to attempt anything of a siege; This decision, indeed, so necessarily results from the present evident appearance of everything around us, that it excites no astonishment, and no disappointment

I am sorry, however, to add that Sir R. Strachan, according to report, does not approve of it. He is of opinion that the ships should at least be allowed to make an attempt. He declined to attend the Council, and, it is said, has appealed to the Government at home for further orders. Every land officer, however, concurs in opinion with the reported decision of the Council. The French have made the most extraordinary efforts. It is really wonderful with what expedition they have assembled a force in every quarter. Bernadotte is certainly at Antwerp, and Dumonceau in Cadsand. The latter island is covered with encampments, and batteries surround the coast.

Such, therefore, is the present state of our military affairs— the French in great and increasing strength, and our own commanders in doubt and division. By division you must not infer that I intend any reflection on any parties concerned. I am persuaded that everything has been done that was possible to be done; that Flushing could not have been taken before the batteries were opened, and the ships brought round; that, by reason of the roads and the weather, the batteries could not have been ready before the 11th; and that, by reason of the wind, the ships could not have got round till the evening of the same and following day. The bombardment therefore could not have been made before it actually was.

As to the question, whether Flushing might not have been left behind? I am of a decided opinion that, in common prudence, it should not. The success of Sir John Hope at Goes was not expected. At any rate, how was he to have proceeded without shipping? And if he had taken the shipping, what would have become of the siege of Flushing? Flushing would have held out till doomsday against a mere land-force. The shipping were wanted for Lillo, and could not be at both places at once. Flushing was first in order, and therefore it was necessary to wait till this impediment was removed. Everything has certainly been done that was possible.

However unpleasant may be our present situation, it neither relaxes our efforts, nor our demonstrations of further intentions. Everything appears as if we were immediately about to proceed to Antwerp. The transports and the ships of war have weighed for the West Scheldt, and the sailors go off with cheers, under the persuasion that they are to burn, or bring off the French fleet. I am afraid, however, that they will be disappointed in their expectations.

The immense force assembled at Cadsand has excited great alertness in the garrison of Flushing. Within the last few days the picquets and sentries have been doubled; and orders have been given to the sentinels, to direct a vigilant attention to the ships of war off in the roadstead, and that if blue rockets were discharged from any of them, a communication was to be immediately made to the commanding officer, General Picton. The acknowledged motive for issuing these orders is the apprehension of an attack from the enemy who, to the number of

13,000 men are in Cadsand, under the command of Bernadotte, for the avowed object; of recovering this island.—Within these few days three hundred gun-boats have reached that place from Boulogne, through the canals; and I assure you it is the decided conviction of some of the most intelligent inhabitants, that the attempt will certainly be made. Bernadotte's military fame is committed by his master upon the issue. At all events, the brigade stationed here, consisting of the 36th, the 63rd, and 77th Regiments, with the Honourable Colonel Cochrane's battalion of embodied ,detachments, are kept upon the alert, which, together with the positions taken by our ships of war, afford to us the most confident hopes that the enemy may repent his temerity, notwithstanding the opportunity which the damaged condition of the batteries of this fortress may at this moment present to them.

The duty of this garrison is likewise very severe, every regiment being obliged to furnish, independent of the necessary guards, parties of 150 and 200 men, to dismantle the works which were constructed for its bombardment. The works are to be immediately put into, a more complete state of defence, and 100 additional guns are to be placed on the ramparts at Flushing. Such an intention indicates the determination of making Walcheren a depôt, from which British manufactures may always find their way to the Continent.

A very considerable discovery of concealed French property has been lately made in Middleburg, by the assiduity of the commissioners; not only specie to a very large amount, but many tons of valuable goods have been ferreted out. The ingenuity of the French, both in plundering, and in concealing their plunder, is beyond all example. In Lisbon, Junot being compelled by the Cintra Convention to restore all plundered property., with the exception of specie, secretly erected some mints, and coined the church plate into French silver and gold money.

The French property now discovered, was claimed by the smugglers as private property. If your prize-laws were better arranged and administered, our spirits would have been elevated under the expectation of rich stores; but it seems that the navy are to have their share, and therefore that the business is to go before the courts. Intelligence has just been received that Sir Home Popham has fought a series of skirmishes with the flotilla of the enemy, and has compelled them to retire under Fort Lillo. The following is the return which has been made of the actual strength of the French fleet:—

Albanois	74	*Duguesclin.*	74
Anversais	74	*Friedland*	74
Audacieux	74	*Henri*	74
Charlemagne	74	*Josephine*	74
Commerce de Lyons	74	*Pultusk*	74
Dalmatia	74	*Thesée*	74
Dantzic	74	*Ville de Berlin*	74

With four frigates, several corvettes, and a great number of gun-boats.

They have all passed Fort Lillo. Before they can be approached, the immense chain and boom which are across the river, must be broken, and the Fort of Lillo must be passed. The chain is, I understand, considerably larger, and more difficult to be broken, than that which crossed Basque roads. The attempt to break it was to have been made, and probably has been before now, by the *Courageux*, Captain Plampin. The distance between Lillo and Fort de Liefkenshoch is not half a mile.

It is now ascertained that the French ships may pass Antwerp, and render it necessary to take that city before they can be destroyed.

General Monnet and his suite will have reached England before you have received this. The character of Monnet I have already mentioned; he is very much disliked, and is said to have been over cautious of his own person during the bombardment. This .however, I do not believe, as the whole character of his defence of the town is brave, and he might certainly have surrendered it at any moment. No one speaks well of the fallen, and particularly where he has not used his power in the most moderate degree.

Amongst the English papers which have reached us, some of them, I find, have been unjust enough to reflect upon the Marquis of Huntley for not having landed on Cadsand. It was certainly a part of the original plan to take possession of this island; and the Marquis of Huntley's division was appointed to this service. The Marquis of Huntley, however, after hovering about the coast, deemed it prudent not to attempt a landing, not because it would have been difficult to have possessed himself of it, but because it would have been impossible to have retained it.

The force in Cadsand exceeded six thousand men, and the sea-boats could not have landed more than 700 of our men in one tide. What then would have been the probable circumstances of these 700 men, exposed during so many hours to the attack of as many thousands? The point of fact, moreover, is, that the gut between Cadsand and Flanders is so extremely narrow, that the French can at any time pass it; and as they can necessarily bring a superior force, all that we could have done, would have been of little avail. It is very easy to remark at home, and censure our military motions; but everything, of this kind depends so much upon circumstances, that it is a flagrant injustice to decide without them.

As to the question whether Flushing might not have been left behind, one circumstance alone is to me decisive. If Flushing had been left behind, or merely blockaded by land, the enemy could have poured any strength into it from Cadsand; in a word, they could shortly have rendered it an over-match for that part of our force which we could have spared for the blockade. Your papers, however, say, "Could there not have been a naval blockade?"

Certainly; but in that case what ships and boats were there left for the attack of Lillo, and the forts between Lillo and Antwerp. Flushing was, in fact, taken by the ships, rather than by the, army, and, these ships were equally wanted for Lillo and the forts.

The same paper asks, if Flushing could not have been taken by a *coup-de-main?* If anything be the extreme of absurdity, it is this question. A town regularly fortified, and, to give you an idea of it at once, with walls nearly as high as those of the King's Bench Prison in England. It is true that the 82nd Regiment had a very brave affair almost under the walls on the night following our landing; but they were not mad enough to have attempted entering the town. The gates were, in fact, closed long before they reached the fosse; and a number of the enemy were killed, from the caution of the garrison guard in admitting the fugitives into the town. Surely nothing but the very spirit of party could have produced such a question.

There appear to me but these two possible questions: in the first place, whether the expedition could have been followed up without taking Flushing and Walcheren? And in the second place, whether any time has been lost in taking Flushing? To both of these I reply in the negative, It was necessary to take Flushing, in order to prevent the enemy from assembling in superior strength on our rear, and thus, in the event of our failure, to have ruined us most completely. And no time has certainly been lost in taking Flushing; because Flushing could only have been taken by the ships, and the ships could not come round till the wind served, that is to say, not till the 11th and 12th.

It is but justice to add, in our own defence, that if there can be any blame attached to the expedition (remember, I give no opinion), it belongs to the Government at home, rather than either to the army or the navy; and you would act more fairly at home, if in all these cases you separated the one from the other. Nothing is more cruel and more unjust than party attacks on the military.

Whilst we are exposing our lives for you, we cannot but think you ungrateful when you repay us only with scorn and sneers. I hope we shall have no more of this. As to a court martial or a court of enquiry, it appears to us ridiculous in the extreme: I repeat, that everything has been done which by any possibility could have been done; and that even if the immediate return of the army, which you so precipitately anticipate, should occur, you will have to thank, rather than to inculpate, our commander in chief. You form your judgement without any knowledge of the circumstances. So much I am enabled positively to state, that General Hope has declared that nothing further can be done, and that the expedition should immediately return, retaining Walcheren only till the pleasure of the Government be known.

Two very important questions appear to me to arise from the present state of things—how far Walcheren may be retained? And whether it will answer any purpose to retain it? With respect to the possibility of retaining Walcheren, it will certainly be very difficult, if not impracticable. It is commanded by the opposite coast of Beveland; and any batteries erected there, can certainly reach this island. The interval is greater between Cadsand and Walcheren; but it will require a strong naval force, and a constant vigilance, to prevent the enemy from landing even from Cadsand.

Under these circumstances, I am really apprehensive that a greater force will be required to keep Walcheren than our Government can spare for that single purpose. In winter, moreover, the Dutch coast is dangerous in the extreme; and as we experienced on our first arrival, our ships cannot be worked in all winds. Campveer is within cannon-shot of South Beveland; and the enemy can pass from the East Scheldt into Beveland at their pleasure. It is certain, moreover, that they will spare no effort to retake this island, not so much on account of its actual worth, as that it appeals to their pride and point of honour. Under these circumstances, it is my opinion that they can bring a greater force to bear against the island, than we can afford to oppose to them.

As to the value of Walcheren, it is either absolute or relative. Its absolute value, its value as a possession in itself, is nothing; it is certainly apt equal to its own maintenance, and still less to the support of a large garrison. If you keep it, therefore, you must send sufficient corn from England to support not merely your own soldiery but the inhabitants.

As to the relative value of Walcheren; it is equally on the negative side. It cannot neutralize the flotilla, or fleet of the enemy: it cannot prevent them from entering or leaving the Scheldt at their pleasure.

After having said so much, it is necessary, I should suppose, to add, it is my decided opinion that Walcheren ought not to be retained. It has ever been a principle with me never to persist in a bad speculation, under the expectation that anything will arise to amend it. More is gained by shifting with the wind, than by trying to make good a course against it.

Yours &c

Letter 13

Campveer, August 30, 1809.

My Dear Friend,

Everything is at length determined, and we are about to re-embark for England. The decision in the grand Council of War held in Beveland, has been that, from the immense force collected by the French in all quarters, and more particularly at Lillo and Antwerp, nothing further is to be done; and the force being too great merely to retain Walcheren, that all the supernumerary part of it shall be sent home. I understand, moreover, that this resolution has been adopted without a dissentient voice. The naval officers did not attend the Council; Sir Richard Strachan did not deem himself a party concerned, and therefore declined the invitation to assist in the deliberations.

The efforts made by the French have indeed been very extraordinary. Bernadotte is in Cadsand with at least 20,000 men. Dumonceau is at Brussels with the same number, and Kellerman is advancing from the Weser. There is a report, likewise, that the garrison of Paris and the intermediate towns are marching against us; add to all this, that the country is flooded nearly two feet deep in water, and you may readily conceive that the difficulties to further progress are insurmountable.

Orders have been issued, that the re-embarkation, from Beveland is to commence tomorrow; and it is not disguised that

Beveland is to be evacuated within four days. The French in the meantime keep hovering over us on the opposite bank of the Scheldt, and occasionally shew their teeth; but have too much prudence to come near enough to bite.

Fortunately for our men, our transports are at hand. Unfortunately, however, there is a miserable absence, of all comfort and accommodation on board these hired vessels.

The captains think that they perform their contract if they stow our men like so many goods wherever they will lie; they are accordingly thrown together like so many packages, and the motion of the sea, and the consequent commotion of their stomachs, render them as motionless and inanimate.

Nothing can possibly be more miserable than the spectacle which is presented in a crowded transport. Imagine some hundreds of human creatures lying as thick together as tamarinds in a jar; here a hand, there a foot, there a face forcing itself above the shoulders of the crowd, in order to collect a breath of air, and there the uplifted hands of another plucking him down, in order that his own face may have a turn; when suddenly the vessel gives a roll, and everyone is seized in an instant with the most horrible sickness.

All these are images which every minute meet your eyes. The cries of the women and children, for we have but too many of them, add to the horror of the scene. You can scarcely conceive the horrible effect which the shortest voyage in one of these transports produces in the health, as well as in the appearance of our men. The exhaustion from the heat, the sickness and the fatigue are so great, that when our poor fellows are first landed, they cannot stand on their feet. They throw themselves down on the sands, and no importunity or command can move them. Some of them are consigned instantly to the surgeon, and many of them never recover. The voyage usually costs us as much as the battle; and I am persuaded that all of us to a man would rather incur the risk of the enemy than the certain evils of the other.

I am sorry to have to add, that the contagious nervous and

putrid fever daily gain ground; and that, unless something can be done to arrest its progress, and to diminish its virulence, disease alone will compel us to abandon our conquest. It is acknowledged by everyone to whom I have ever mentioned the subject, that the English soldiers suffer, more by changes of climate; and by any unusual privations or feverishes of any kind, than the soldiers of any other European nation. We catch colds and fevers as if we were so many women; and those colds and fevers prove fatal to us in a greater proportion. Enquire of your medical friends, whether they can assign any satisfactory reason for this unfortunate difference. The French do not suffer one tenth part in the wear and tear of a campaign; whereas a few days' rain or a soaking mist will invalid a whole British army.

The medical returns of this day are very disheartening. Not a regiment is there but what has suffered in a greater or less degree, and some of them so excessively, as to be sent to the hospital by companies. This has been the case with the 23rd; the whole of which, with the exception of about fifty men, is in the hospital. On yesterday's parade they were excused from all further duty, and reported in the hospital.

Nearly one half of the 36th regiment are in the same condition, and four hundred men of the 26th. The 71st and 84th have likewise suffered most severely; and if the progress of the disease continue, and it seems likely to do so, not a man will remain for garrison service. The attack is generally very sudden, being preceded by a common cold. The dysentery and cholera *morbus* are certainly contagious; and if every care were not taken to ensure cleanliness, a still greater number would have been swept off.

Many of our officers have likewise been seized with the typhus fever; and one general remark has been made, that no cold in this island is harmless. The damp seems, in the first place, to open the pores, and then to penetrate them. You can really feel it as it is penetrating into your vitals. Your climate in England is variable enough in all conscience; but this of Walcheren is inconstancy itself. We have not had two fine days together since we left England. Even our warm weather is but a muggy damp and a hot fog.

Even the rains, however, in one point of view, may be considered as fortunate. There is such a dearth of springs in this island, that the inhabitants have not fresh water enough for their use. The French garrison used to send boats a considerable distance down the Scheldt, to supply them with this necessary. All the water hereabouts is spoiled by the sea. If there had been no rain, therefore, our troops would have wanted water.

Our physicians and surgeons are employed in endeavours to investigate the cause of the diseases which threaten to annihilate us. They seem to me to resolve themselves into one very simple point, the putrid exhalations, and penetrating damps. Wherever there is a hot fog, there will always be a putrid contagion. This is the case in South America; it is the case in the West Indies; it is the case in every country in the world in similar circumstances. Whence is it, for example, that even in England the spring and fall are notoriously the most unhealthy parts of the year? It is only because the increasing heat of the sun, and the damps of the earth, are concurrent; the one opens the pores, and the other enters them.

It is reported here that, as it is not in our power to reach the French fleet, we are to endeavour to render it useless by sinking hulks, &c. in the mouth of the river. It is certainly very possible to sink these vessels; but there is one material point, and that is, that the enemy can raise them at less cost than we can sink them. They could only be prevented from so doing by batteries raised along the banks of the Scheldt; and as we cannot maintain these batteries, the attempt to impede the navigation by these means will be in vain.

To say all in a word, the expedition has failed, but has not failed from any fault in the military. Flanders is proverbially the strongest part of the French dominions; and it really surprises me that this part should have been selected for a point of attack. Our Government have been flagrantly deceived.

The army under General Hope in Beveland have suffered nearly as much as the division in Walcheren by disease. The cause, as I have said, is in the air; and wherever that reaches, we may expect the effect. Our men, even such as are in health, have the features of so many walking corpses; everyone wishes to be at home, and everyone without disguise begins to express this wish.

You will naturally ask whether our reverse of fortune, for such it is, has produced any difference in our Dutch friends. None in the least. They endured us from the beginning, and they endure us still. They look passively on, contenting themselves with an expressive shake of the head whilst they see us riding over their fields. A Dutchman, of whatever degree, in feature, in mind, and in deportment, resembles an English country overseer; he is silent, and sullen; nothing can awe him into civility, and he seems to regard every stranger as a vagrant.

Middleburg, however, still continues very pleasant; the shops are gay, and constitute our morning lounge, and the rooms, as we call them, are open in the evening. The nature and use of these rooms; will astonish you. In the first place, all the fashionable and respectable families in the island, sons, daughters, mothers, and fathers, assemble there; the rooms are well lighted, and the music and. dancing good.

So far you will say that there is nothing extraordinary; but what will you think, when I inform you that these rooms are actually the public room's, the exhibition rooms of a *bagnio*, that the dancers are the stock in trade, of the tavern-keeper, and that his profits arise from what they receive nightly for their favours. These girls are all kept in the house; they are boarded at the expense of the tavern-keeper, and are supplied by him with clothes. Twice or thrice in the week the rooms are open, and the girls made to exhibit themselves in dancing. There is nothing thought of visiting these places; everyone does it: so much do manners differ. The Dutch, the gravest people in the world, vindicate these institutions, and permissive *bagnios*, upon the argument that such practices must be, and therefore that it is better to regulate what they cannot altogether prevent.

Flushing is not near so gay a town as Middleburg; it rather

resembles Plymouth, except that the characteristic cleanliness of the Dutch gives it an air of neatness in despite of its trade and fishery. Middleburg, moreover, has some regular and respectable assemblies, which Flushing has not. Flushing is a town of smugglers and fishermen; in Middleburg the citizens have been smugglers, but have now left off business.

The Dutch have no ideas of dramatic performance. There is indeed something of a theatre at Middleburg, but it is not open. The Dutch ideas of a play do not arise above a puppet-shew; these have something answering to our Punch, but even Punch seems there to lose his drollery. In England the dramatic of Punch and Joan abounds in our characteristic humour. In Holland this humour is merely manual, and that of the grossest kind. In Italy, Punch appears in the dress and shape of Scaramouch, and is said to be more witty than in England. Some vagabond strollers, as I have been informed, visit Middleburg in the beginning of the summer. I have endeavoured to collect some knowledge as to their performances.

The Dutch, I believe, have no comedies which have been reduced to writing; they have dialogues and pantomimes, but there is no unity of action, no connected fable, without which there can be no drama. The Dutch seem to want those nicer powers of the understanding to which wit and humour appeal. In solid learning the Dutch have, equalled any nation in Europe; but, with the exception of Erasmus, and one or two more illustrious names, they cannot produce a distinguished writer. It would be unpardonable, indeed, not to except Boerhaave from this national character—a man whom our own Dr. Johnson thus characterized:

> A man formed by nature for great designs, and guided by religion in the exertion of his abilities. Determined to lose none of his hours, when he had attained one science, he attempted another; he added physic to divinity, chemistry to the mathematics, and anatomy to botany. He recommended truth by his elegance, and embellished the philosopher with polite literature; yet his knowledge, however

uncommon, holds in his character but the second place, for his virtue was more uncommon than his learning. He ascribed all his abilities to the bounty, and all his goodness tor the grace of his God. May those who study his writings, imitate his life; and those who endeavour after his knowledge, aspire likewise to his piety!

Have I at any time mentioned to you the incredible quantity of coffee which the Dutch consume? Nothing so soon meets the eye of an Englishman when visiting a Dutch family. If he call in the morning, coffee and roasted fish are served to him, as a passing refreshment. After dinner, coffee is in greater plenty than wine. The Dutch I am persuaded could sooner dispense with spirits than with coffee. It is not drunk so sweet as in England, but is infinitely better. On the other hand, tea is scarce, and is very bad. It seems scarce, however, only because it is not required for the Dutch warehouses abound to an astonishing degree with every article of Indian produce. England does not enjoy a monopoly of this trade to so great an extent as is thought; or at least her monopoly does not reach the Continent.

The Dutch, I believe, still contrive to carry on an important trade with China through the neutral medium of America. I do not say this from any grudge towards a neutral flag; they are convenient to both parties, and limit the natural evils of war. Nothing, in my humble opinion, is more absurd than the excessive clamour which the political writers in England have excited upon this point. As a commercial nation, we must lose infinitely more than we gain by this liberty of the neutral medium.

As we are about to leave this country, I shall endeavour to throw together all the information I have been enabled to collect. You must take it, however, in mass, as I have not the time to give it order and arrangement.

The Dutch of this island, and I believe of all Holland, are particularly fond of their gardens; so much so, that there is scarcely a house in the towns but what has some garden attached to it without the walls. In the Middleburg road there are some of these gardens on both sides. Hither such of the inhabitants as have not country houses, repair in the evenings of summer and autumn, and give and receive entertainments of tea and coffee. The amusements of a Dutchman exactly correspond with those of a London cockney. They seem to have precisely the same ideas of comfort, and their elegance and luxury are on the same scale.

Sometimes, where the garden is too highly rented for the finances of one family, two or three will club together, in which case the gardens become common to the respective families. Never do any people enjoy their pleasures with more silence and gravity. The women take their tea and coffee with the dignity of so many statesmen in solemn congress; the men smoke; if any one party meet another party, they exchange salutations, but very seldom any conversation. A Dutchman is as careful of his words as of his money. He seems to deem it an inexcusable folly to converses on subjects which do not belong to him; and nothing in his own opinion, concerns him, unless it attach immediately to himself or his family.

The Dutch Jews have a custom peculiar to themselves; they bury their dead at some distance from the towns or villages. The churches and churchyards are sacred to the use of the Christians; and so far as religious moderation is carried, the Catholics very frequently bury their dead in Protestant Churches. So much of the ancient prejudices against the Jews still remain, that the Christians refuse to be associated with them, either living or dead. The new law may gradually eradicate these feelings; but as things are at present, the Jews, though they are tolerated, are still kept a distinct people. In burials in Walcheren, moreover, the national and characteristic economy is strikingly displayed. Everyone is interred in the most simple manner possible; and a Dutchman is always ready with the observation that an expensive funeral may injure the living, and cannot in any way serve the dead.

In every town or village in Walcheren, the registers are preserved as so many valuable records. The births, deaths, and marriages are there duly recorded, as in England. The use of these kind of parish annals has been often experienced in our Courts of Justice. In England I believe the practice is not very ancient; in Walcheren it would seem to be coeval with the inhabitants of the island.

Walcheren has likewise its poor-laws and poor-rates, in the same manner as we have them in England. Every town and village maintains its own poor; and the important task of supervision and distribution is not left to the ignorance and cruelty of an individual overseer. All the respectable housekeepers are formed into council, who manage everything connected with the support, and active and public employment of their own poor,

Middleburg cannot boast of any literary institutions, though there are many individuals who have both wealth, and leisure, and inclination for literary pursuits. There are some booksellers' shops, however, and before the landing of the English, there were some papers in the French and Dutch languages. Since our arrival a speculator has established a new journal. Very little, however, can be said in its favour. The Dutch are still half a century behind the English.

They talk here that the King of Holland is about to divide the States into departments, in order to assist the projected measure of a military conscription. The present military force of Holland amounts to about 60,000 men, cavalry and infantry. From the immense population of the country, which is evident even to a cursory visitant, I make no doubt but that this amount can be doubled or trebled; and whatever can be done, will most assuredly be done by Bonaparte: it is the characteristic nature of this man that he pushes the capability of everything to its utmost; he will make the most of everything. He is almost the only conqueror in modern times, who has contrived to incorporate the conquered nations into his efficient armies.

Travelling in Walcheren and throughout Flanders seems to be very cheap and very convenient. The farmers let their horses in the same manner as the livery stable-keepers in England. The Flemish coaches are awkward in the extreme; they resemble what were common in England fifty years since. It really astonishes me that two horses can drag them along the Dutch roads. If I had a draughtsman at hand, I would send you a landscape, in which the whole island should be reduced so as to form one picture. You can scarcely imagine how novel the scenery would be.

The many spires and chimneys of the villages rising above the trees and coppices; the minute divisions and compartments of the lands; the numerous cottages and farmhouses, some white, some red, some new, some very ancient, some covered with vines, and some with painted shutters, altogether compose a spectacle of happy industry and contented mediocrity which appeal strongly to the heart and the feelings. The Dutch laws spare no pains to prevent the consolidation of small farms into one overgrown property: the consequence is, that Walcheren is very thickly inhabited, and almost in every hole and corner is cultivated like a garden. This system, however, has its inconvenience; but as Holland has many vents for any excess of population, it has not as yet experienced them.

The most heavy tax in Walcheren, and throughout Holland, is the land-tax, which amounts, I believe, or rather did amount, to one fourth of the actual rent. In England you are rated low, and taxed highly. In Walcheren, and throughout Holland, they are rated at the actual rent, and are taxed highly into the bargain. There was likewise another very obnoxious tax—a tax on cattle and stock. The consequence of this impost was, that the farmers necessarily restricted themselves in the value and extent of their stock, and their land suffered in proportion. Be the necessities of the State ever so great, the legislator should make a long pause before he assails the root of all increase and of all source of taxation.

I know not whether in any of my letters I have made any remarks on the Dutch system of agriculture. As far as I can deduce any conclusions from Walcheren, they are inferior to the English as practical farmers. In England alone agriculture is at once a science and a practice. Your numerous Boards of Agriculture, your books, and your experimental farms have gradually ameliorated the English practice, and in despite of the almost invincible force of old habits, you have compelled even your farmers to adopt modern improvements.

In Walcheren there is nothing of this; the consequence is, that the old system continues, and there is no trace of any progressive amelioration. Walcheren most probably has always been what it is now. The minute division of the lands has given a kind of gardenlike cultivation to every spot in the neighbourhood of the towns; but where the farms are larger, they are all managed on the old fallowing system. They have no idea of the alternate succession of corn and pulse, or roots. Every man follows the practice of his father, and everyone is contented if he can gain the same crops.

There is in Walcheren, however, none of that mongrel race of men between gentlemen and farmers, who are the disgrace of England, and who, without the education and manners of gentlemen, ape all their follies and even their vices. You will not see in Walcheren the farmer seated at the head of a luxurious and expensive table, passing about the bottle, and accompanying it with coarse and blasphemous ribaldry.

You will not see the farmer's daughter returning from market with a maid behind her overloaded with the last importation of licentious novels. This species of books is indeed scarcely known in Holland; and if the Dutch are half a century behind us in their knowledge, they are equally so in their vices. Here are no milkmaids flaunting about in muslin gowns; no yeomen's daughters educated at an expensive boarding-school, and returning home, in the season of the vacation, to execrate their vulgar parents. The Dutch are a simple, unaffected people, and the manners of the lower classes correspond with their stations in life.

The general average of the farms in Holland is from fifty to sixty acres. By a careful and industrious, if not a scientific, cultivation of this portion, the Dutch farmer contrives to live in ease and happiness; his kitchen is full of substantial comforts and rural luxuries; himself and his family have warm clothes to their backs; and if he has any daughters, he contrives to save enough to assist his sons-in-law to establish themselves in farms. He has no ambition to make them gentlemen or gentlewomen.

He educates them for the sphere for which he intends them; and having no ideas above it, they are contented in it. Nothing can be more gratifying than the comfortable spectacles which their farmhouses present: the house is neat both outside and in the garden, the orchard, the paddock, in front and behind, are all fantastically ornamented; turf-seats, arbours, and flowers are in every part and corner. Even the animals have an air of plenty and content—they are fat, sleek, and heavy. Everything about a Dutchman, indeed, has somewhat of a Dutch air.

My former opinion of the Dutch has only been confirmed by all that I have lately seen. I think that they bear a nearer resemblance to the English than any other nation in the world. A Dutch boor is the counterpart of an English peasant, grave, immovable in his visage and deportment, but withal not wanting in natural benevolence. Their forms, however, have not the same symmetry with those of Englishmen: they are invariably thickset, large headed, and broad shoulders. Their women have complexions not inferior to those of my country women; but they want their animation and their intelligence.

In England only do the minds of women seem on a par with those of men. In a Dutch assembly the point of manners amongst the women is to maintain an invincible silence, and a fixed reserve. They never mingle in the conversation except when they whisper their husbands or brothers. A Dutch girl, however, is not without the feelings natural to her sex; however frozen maybe their reception of strangers, they doubly welcome their accepted lovers with the characteristic tenderness of their age and sex. Our officers, however, have not to boast much of their favours.

By all that I have seen, I have no hesitation to say that, next to my own countrymen, the Dutch appear to me the most moral and religious nation on the face of the globe, and are therefore the most valuable men. The men, even in a humid climate, are examples of a rigid sobriety; and the women, even in despite of the contagion of French example, are chaste, ingenuous, and unaffected. A Dutch Lutheran Church, in the simplicity and neatness of its appearance, resembles an English Quakers' meeting; the faces of the women are concealed, under modest bonnets, and if you at any time catch their eyes, they receive your gaze with the innocence and unconcern of children; they look at you till their curiosity is satisfied, and then revert to the preacher and the prayer-book.

Luxury has happily not as yet found its way into Walcheren. I do think that: there are not more than three or four coaches in the whole island; and I am persuaded that there is no individual who in house expenses lives at the rate of one thousand a year.

If Walcheren should be retained, and can be retained, it might become a comfortable asylum to such of your countrymen whom narrow circumstances may compel to look out for cheapness, united with some degree of comfort. In its natural circumstances, that is to say, when without an army, Walcheren is infinitely cheaper than any part of England and Wales. In Walcheren, moreover, such families might find their own religion. I have before said that every form of religion is tolerated, and Lutheranism is in chief favour. In Walcheren, also, there is a purity of morals, and a rational and cheerful piety, which could not fail to please every properly instructed mind.

Confess that, during my stay in this island, I have not forgotten your request to be particular, even to minuteness. I shall perhaps be enabled to write you another letter. Everything, however, is now preparing for our departure; for that no orders have as yet been given, but they are expected every moment. The intention of abandoning all further attempts on the enemy's forts and shipping has indeed, been publicly announced.

Yours &c.

LETTER 14

September 8, 1809.
My Dear Friend,

We are under orders of re-embarkation the day after tomorrow. This is, then, the last letter you will receive, and I shall therefore endeavour to sum up in it all that may interest you.

In one of the letters which have reached me from you, you make some enquiries as to the Dutch literature and language. I believe that I have already informed you that Walcheren is not only deficient in every literary appearance, but that there are no apparent means in Walcheren of any possibility of obtaining anything beyond the most common information. The Dutch in Walcheren seem to have but two purposes—that of making, and that of enjoying their fortunes.

One half of them is occupied in the former, and such as have yet their fortunes to make, are too active in the pursuit of them, to have any leisure for literary pursuits. It does therefore appear to me not only that Holland is not the country of learned men, but that it never will be. There seems no hereditary wealth—no one is born to a large fortune. The property of a Dutchman is divided amongst his children; and as, in one or two generations, the original capital thus subdivided, must become very small, everyone has the same necessary object with his ancestors, to make their fortunes, and meddle only with their own concerns.

The Dutch, however, have one institution which seems well calculated to encourage learning, by inciting emulation. This is a public examination of all the youth in the public schools. This examination is usually held in the body of the great church. Twice every year, on certain appointed days, the whole city are invited to view this spectacle. The boys are seated in the body of the church, or town-house, whilst the rector, the magistrates, and the spectators are ranged around them.

The assembly is opened by a short speech in favour and praise of literature, after which the most distinguished of the youth are called forward, and each of them undergoes the appointed examination. Such of them, as are about to commence a regular professional course at the University, are expected to distinguish themselves by a. speech in praise of Erasmus, who, to the honour of Dutch taste and Dutch gratitude, still continues their literary star. It is scarcely possible but that this inculcated admiration of so eminent a man must be productive of the most beneficial effects. Examples must have the same power in learning as in morals; and it cannot be possible so long and so attentively to study, and to contemplate the bright exemplar of an eminent man, without catching some of that kindred spirit which rendered him what he was.

After the examination is past, the prizes of eloquence and science are distributed. These consist of books highly ornamented. Happy are those who can obtain these prizes; their fame is fixed during their lives; for the whole States so nearly resemble a private family, that what passes in any one place is immediately circulated throughout.

The Dutch and the Chinese, I believe, are the only nations in the world who seem to make learning of any public importance; and yet, strange to say, both Dutch and Chinese continue very backward in the general progress of the Arts and Sciences. Holland is where it was in the days of Erasmus, and China has scarcely moved since the era of Confucius.

There is another point connected with the literary state of the Dutch, which should not be passed over. If the Dutch cannot pretend to any decisive figure amongst the *literati* of the day, they do not neglect at least the elementary part of education; they do not pass over the foundation of morals, and of the conduct of life. If Holland have few academics, she has many schools, and everyone can at least read.

The first care of the State has evidently been the instruction of youth. The Dutch seem to consider that no one can be a good citizen unless he is enabled to know his duties, and understand the force of his obligations. This most useful part of learning, therefore, if so it may be called, is diffused over Holland still more generally than over England.

A Dutchman unable to read, would be a phenomenon. They have no such complete vagabonds as to belong to a nation without understanding its language. This kind of education, moreover, seems to produce the same effects in the Dutch States as in

Scotland. It is a general observation in England, that the Scotch are infinitely more moral than the English, and that the criminal lists in Scotland have fewer examples of depravity than the same lists in England.

The same observations will apply to the Dutch States, as compared with those of their more ignorant neighbours. The Dutch and the Swiss, in point of moral conduct, are infinitely superior to any other of the Continental nations; and for the evident reason, that they are better, and more generally informed. It may be a doubt whether the lower classes of society should have more than a certain degree of education; but it is to the interest of every nation that the whole of its people should have sufficient information to read, and understand their civil and individual duties.

The Dutch language seems, very ill adapted to the attainment of any eminence in poetry or eloquence. It consists of more guttural words than any other language since the tower of Babel. It is the harshest part of the German sounds. King Charles said well of it, that he would talk English to his friends, Italian to his mistress, and Dutch to his horse. I do not know whether the Dutch have any native poets, but I should rather think that they have none.

They have certainly none of any eminence, or we should have heard of them. Every nation has heard something of our Milton, Shakespeare, and Dryden; but I have never heard of any Dutch epic or dramatic poet. This is conclusive evidence with me that there are none. Poetry is so much in favour with mankind, that even the Dutch language would not long have concealed any eminent genius.

This language, however, has a very near resemblance to the English. It is related of Dr. Johnson, that, by way of making trial of the state of his memory when an old man, he attempted to learn the High Dutch language; and finding that he could with much ease retain the words after having once had recourse for them to the dictionary, he became satisfied with himself, and laid aside the study. It is well observed by the relator of this anecdote, that the similarity of the Dutch and English languages, and of many of the words of each, is so great, that the doctor was perhaps too easily satisfied as to his powers of memory; for that the Dutch word would very frequently point out the English word with which it corresponded in frame and meaning. This similarity is certainly so very great as to become a strong argument of a connate origin. Many of the Dutch words are English in everything but their termination.

As to your other question, whether Walcheren can be retained, in my opinion, as I have before stated, I do not think that it can. Walcheren can only be retained by a force of from 10,000 to 15,000 men; and you can best say whether, under all circumstances, you can afford such a force. Beveland is commanded from the East Scheldt, whence an enemy on the Continent can pass at their pleasure. And, in my humble opinion, Walcheren is equally commanded by Beveland, inasmuch as the distance is so small between Campveer and Beveland, that the one is within cannon-shot of the other.

If the enemy therefore should pass into Beveland, they will find but little difficulty in effecting a passage thence to Walcheren. On the Cadsand side the danger is still greater. The distance is almost the same, and the water so shallow, and so enclosed from the action of winds, that our ships cannot act to prevent them. Upon the whole, it is the general opinion of the military, that the French can retake this, island, whenever they may deem it advisable to send an army of thirty thousand men against it.

The retention of this island must certainly be peculiarly mortifying to the Emperor Napoleon, as the object of the attack of it was to destroy one of his favourite schemes in its very formation. Whatever therefore can be done to effect the recovery of it, will be done. It is a part of the character of Bonaparte to have recourse to no half measures; he owes indeed, half his success to his determined resolution, and to his obstinate pursuit of a purpose once adopted. If he be resolved, therefore, to have Walcheren, England I am afraid cannot keep it from him.

There is another very important consideration. If Walcheren

be kept, it must not only be defended, but it must be fed by England. I question whether, from your present harvest, this will not be a point of more moment than it will seem. You will say, perhaps, that you would equally have to keep your soldiers, whether at home or abroad. This reasoning is not just, as you would confess, if you once saw the method of military supply. You have to supply not only their consumption, but their waste, the necessary waste of the transit, the removal, and the quantity spoiled.

The amount of this exceeds all computation. You might feed an army of thirty five thousand men abroad with a less expense than, an army of ten thousand men would cost you at home. It is this circumstance which renders the price of corn so much dearer in a season of war than in peace. The supply of distant garrisons takes off near one tenth of the whole quantity brought to the market.

If Walcheren, moreover, be kept, you will have to incur another necessary expense, that of supplying it with water. The water of the island cannot be drunk with safety. It is brackish and hard; it is scarcely fit even for any culinary purpose. The Dutch inhabitants supply themselves from very distant quarters. You must bring it from England. Will not the expense of this freightage be a very heavy drawback on the reputed value of the island?

I should not forget the still more serious drawback on your population, to keep up the garrison to its necessary standard. The men are now dying at the average of 250 per week. If this mortality continue, and I am afraid that there is too much reason to reckon that it will continue, what resources will be equal to it? In my humble opinion, as I have frequently before stated, it is more consistent with wisdom to abandon an hopeless project, than by an obstinate perseverance to add error to error, and ultimately perhaps swell the sum of disaster to a serious amount. Obstinacy is more frequently and more extensively mischievous than, the contrary extreme of inconstancy or imbecility.

Putting, all these circumstances together, it does not appear to me that Walcheren can be retained. Nor can I see any useful purpose which would be answered by its retention. It would certainly not serve as a blockade to the French fleet; for, according to all the information that I have been enabled to obtain, the Scheldt cannot be so blockaded, but that the same labour of the enemy would remove the impediment that it would cost us to produce it.

As to sinking, any stone vessels in the channel of the river, they would be of no service, unless at the same time we flank them with protecting batteries. The Emperor of Germany certainly thus choked up the navigation; but the Spaniards had previously erected a line of batteries on each side of the river. Nothing is more evident than that vessels thus sunken, may be removed at pleasure.

Your English papers, as many of them as have reached me, have been very unjust to Lord Chatham. You may believe me that everything has been done which could have been done. There was no possibility of fighting against the obstacles of nature. The climate alone was the best security of the place. When you add to this that the enemy possessed the power of drowning the land at their pleasure, that the mere circumstance of the opening of the sluices, and still more particularly of cutting the dikes, put the country under water for leagues; under all these circumstances I say you will have very little difficulty in acquitting us of having done nothing further.

If anything were impossible, it was to take Flushing by a mere land force, and without a regular siege. We were compelled, therefore, to wait for our heavy artillery; and from the bad state of the roads, and the absolute inutility of our horses, some days were necessarily lost in, this delay. Had it not been for the services of the marines, we should have lost a still longer time. When the heavy artillery was brought up, and the ships came round; the bombardment immediately commenced, and no one will then say that any time was lost.

Nothing can be more contrary than the former and present appearance of our army. Who that was to see us now, would recognise the gay, gallant body of men, who, under the cheering salutations of their countrymen, left Ramsgate about six weeks since, promising themselves those additional laurels which should eclipse, or at least, equal the battles of Maida and Vimeira? In one sense of the word an army is a true mob. A panic spreads through every part of it like an electric spark. They catch the courage, the fear, and the despair of the hour. Nothing can raise them when thoroughly depressed; nothing can depress them whilst rushing precipitately forwards in the career of honour and expectation.

Our poor fellows have learned by some means that they have not equalled the expectations of their countrymen; and under this persuasion I do really believe that they are ashamed to come back. They are as slow in their preparations for re-embarkation as they were brisk and active in their landing. But everything is now changed. They look to a cold reception at home. I should hope, however, that you will not have the injustice to impute the failure of the expedition to any fault of the men. Believe me, in every individual action, and throughout the whole business, they conducted, themselves in a manner worthy of their countrymen.

The Dutch, as I have frequently had occasion to remark, seem very indifferent to all that passes. They look at our preparations with an eye of the most careless regard; they neither smile nor sneer. A Dutchman never forgets himself into anything like sensibility. He is a perfect block, too heavy to be moved by any of those impulses which drive the rest of mankind before them.

On the other hand, the Frenchman is like a feather before the wind; he floats wherever the tide or wind of passion blows. The French prisoners can never conceal their feelings when any reverse happens to them. The grin of pleasure or revenge is then legible in every feature of their face. The Dutchman in prosperity and calamity is equally inanimate. Nothing moves him, nothing pleases him, nothing afflicts him. He is a perfect practical philosopher without knowing it.

Everything is now in such a state of forwardness for our departure, that we are waiting only for the wind. For my part, I have resolved to take example by the Dutch, and, reconciling myself to necessity, make it lighter by bearing it: this is the only true method of alleviating the actual evils of life. There are few of them so bad as riot to be lightened by patience. There is an art in supporting affliction as well as in carrying a burthen: lay it right on your shoulders, and apply yourself manfully to it, and half its oppression is lost.

This is a philosophy which I have lately learned, and it shall hereafter be my guide through life. In this manner has ended an expedition, which in its commencement had excited the most sanguine hopes of the country, and the failure of which must certainly be imputed to some cause either at home or here. I have asserted, and I will maintain, that the army are not to blame; and how far our ministers are to blame at home, is certainly more your cause than mine: under these circumstances, I shall say no more upon the subject.

As to a military enquiry, I think it absurd. There cannot be two opinions on our military operations. Everything, as I have repeatedly stated, has been done that could be done. The first thought of the expedition, of one to the Scheldt, originated in the time of Mr. Pitt General Dumourier was at that time in England, and was consulted upon the occasion.

It was his opinion that such an expedition could not succeed, that the line of the Scheldt was too strong, that a *coup-de-main* was impossible, and that to effect anything by a regular army, would demand too great a force, and a succession of campaigns. It seems to me very extraordinary that, in the face of this opinion, the English Ministry should have persisted in making the attempt. I have no hesitation, however, to say, that I have formed this opinion rather from subsequent events, than from anything which I knew, or could have foreseen, at the time.

I must now conclude. You will shortly see us in England, and I have no doubt but that, in common with your countrymen, you will give us that reception, which our efforts, if our success, have merited.

You will wish, perhaps, to know what is the amount of the

force which is to be left behind to defend Walcheren. The following is the list:—

General Rottenberg's Brigade:
68th Regiment	755 men	439 effective	316 sick
71st Regiment	942 men	603 effective	339 sick
85th Regiment	569 men	437 effective	132 sick

General Allen's Brigade:
1st German Legion	704 men	477 effective	227 sick
2nd ditto	610 men	405 effective	205 sick

Colonel Hay's Brigade:
1st Regiment	934 men	784 effective	150 sick
5th Regiment	914 men	483 effective	431 sick
35th Regiment	730 men	420 effective	310 sick

General Ackland's Brigade:
2nd Regiment	825 men	608 effective	217 sick
76th Regiment	733 men	544 effective	189 sick
32nd Regiment	556 men	365 effective	192 sick

General Dyott's Brigade:
6th Regiment	946 men	450 effective	496 sick
50th Regiment	855 men	523 effective	332 sick
91st Regiment	636 men	431 effective	205 sick

General Brown's Brigade:
23rd Regiment	398 men	154 effective	244 sick
81st Regiment	655 men	463 effective	187 sick
26th Regiment	784 men	548 effective	236 sick

Major General Montresor's Brigade:
36th Regiment	642 men	523 effective	129 sick
38th Regiment	805 men	453 effective	352 sick
77th Regiment	546 men	263 effective	994 sick

50 Royal Staff Corps—160 Wagon Train.
Royal Artillery	1021 men	771 effective	250 sick
Royal Engineers	200 men	150 effective	50 sick

Yours &c.

ALSO FROM LEONAUR
AVAILABLE IN SOFTCOVER OR HARDCOVER WITH DUST JACKET

CAPTAIN OF THE 95th (Rifles) *by Jonathan Leach*—An officer of Wellington's Sharpshooters during the Peninsular, South of France and Waterloo Campaigns of the Napoleonic Wars.

BUGLER AND OFFICER OF THE RIFLES *by William Green & Harry Smith* With the 95th (Rifles) during the Peninsular & Waterloo Campaigns of the Napoleonic Wars

BAYONETS, BUGLES AND BONNETS by *James 'Thomas' Todd*—Experiences of hard soldiering with the 71st Foot - the Highland Light Infantry - through many battles of the Napoleonic wars including the Peninsular & Waterloo Campaigns

THE ADVENTURES OF A LIGHT DRAGOON *by George Farmer & G.R. Gleig*—A cavalryman during the Peninsular & Waterloo Campaigns, in captivity & at the siege of Bhurtpore, India

THE COMPLEAT RIFLEMAN HARRIS *by Benjamin Harris as told to & transcribed by Captain Henry Curling*—The adventures of a soldier of the 95th (Rifles) during the Peninsular Campaign of the Napoleonic Wars

WITH WELLINGTON'S LIGHT CAVALRY *by William Tomkinson*—The Experiences of an officer of the 16th Light Dragoons in the Peninsular and Waterloo campaigns of the Napoleonic Wars.

SURTEES OF THE RIFLES by *William Surtees*—A Soldier of the 95th (Rifles) in the Peninsular campaign of the Napoleonic Wars.

ENSIGN BELL IN THE PENINSULAR WAR *by George Bell*—The Experiences of a young British Soldier of the 34th Regiment 'The Cumberland Gentlemen' in the Napoleonic wars.

WITH THE LIGHT DIVISION *by John H. Cooke*—The Experiences of an Officer of the 43rd Light Infantry in the Peninsula and South of France During the Napoleonic Wars

NAPOLEON'S IMPERIAL GUARD: FROM MARENGO TO WATERLOO by *J. T. Headley*—This is the story of Napoleon's Imperial Guard from the bearskin caps of the grenadiers to the flamboyance of their mounted chasseurs, their principal characters and the men who commanded them.

BATTLES & SIEGES OF THE PENINSULAR WAR by *W. H. Fitchett*—Corunna, Busaco, Albuera, Ciudad Rodrigo, Badajos, Salamanca, San Sebastian & Others

AVAILABLE ONLINE AT **www.leonaur.com**
AND OTHER GOOD BOOK STORES

www.ingramcontent.com/pod-product-compliance
Lightning Source LLC
Chambersburg PA
CBHW021003090426
42738CB00007B/634